WarCraft™ II

Beyond the Dark Portal

METZEN · 95

Official Secrets & Solutions

Now Available

How to Order:

For information on quantity discounts contact the publisher: Prima Publishing, P.O. Box 1260BK, Rocklin, CA 95677-1260; (916) 632-4400. On your letterhead include information concerning the intended use of the books and the number of books you wish to purchase. For individual orders, turn to the back of the book for more information.

WarCraft™ II
Beyond the Dark Portal
Official Secrets & Solutions

Mark Walker

PRIMA PUBLISHING
Rocklin, California
(916) 632-4400

To Heroes Past—my Dad and Ayrton Senna

Heroes Present—my Mom and Janice

Heroes Future—my daughters—Denver, Jessie, and Ayron.

Project Editor: Chris Balmain

All products and characters mentioned in this book are trademarks of their respective companies.

Important:
Prima Publishing, Inc., has made every effort to determine that the information contained in this book is accurate. However, the publisher makes no warranty, either express or implied, as to the accuracy, effectiveness, or completeness of the material in this book; nor does the publisher assume liability for damages, either incidental or consequential, that may result from using the information in this book. The publisher cannot provide information regarding game play, hints and strategies, or problems with hardware or software. Questions should be directed to the support numbers provided by the game and device manufacturers in their documentation. Some game tricks require precise timing and may require repeated attempts before the desired result is achieved.

ISBN: 0-7615-0787-6
Library of Congress Catalog Card Number: 96-68781
Printed in the United States of America

96 97 98 99 HH 10 9 8 7 6 5 4 3 2 1

Contents

Introduction

What's Up With This Game, Anyway?

Real-time strategy gaming in general, and the *Warcraft* series in particular, have become such forces in the computer gaming world it's hard to believe *Warcraft* was released a scant 18 months ago. Since that time, *Warcraft: Orcs & Humans*, and its descendant *Warcraft II: Tides of Darkness*, have sold more than 800,000 copies worldwide. How come?

Certainly *Warcraft* is not the most realistic or graphically stunning strategy game on the market. Yeah, the opening to *Warcraft II* is sharp, but there are better sequences in the industry. And realism? Just what does each Orc, Human, or Death Knight represent? A legion? A cohort? A brigade? For that matter, are the buildings individual structures or representative of a given production capability? Ever wondered about it?

Me neither.

And therein lies the magic. The first time I saw *Star Wars* I didn't question how fighters exploded in space. They shouldn't; there's no air (and we all know you need air for fires and explosions). No, like my little girl's excitement at the shopping-mall when she's shuffled into Santa's weary lap, I was too enthralled to sweat the details. The same goes for Warcraft, the game sucks you in like a sinking Troll Destroyer's vortex. Good media, whether print, film, play, or software, captures its audience, wrapping them in the experience. Once that happens, no one sweats the details. Simply put, *Warcraft* is good media.

Yeah, but why?

Certainly the game's atmosphere has a lot to do with it. Tons of characters with gobs of different abilities all contribute to the game's unique feel. Of course, their retorts when prodded are legendary, so much so that before sending the *Dark Portal* beta to me the folks at Prima booted it up just to "poke the guys and see what they said." That's atmosphere.

Yet all the cool characters in the world won't float a game. The game in its entirety must do that. And the *Warcraft* series does a heck of a job. Game to game, Blizzard keeps its customers guessing. Just when you think you have the hang of building a Town Hall, Farm, Barracks, Kennels, and so on, *Warcraft II* throws a huge monkey wrench in the works, introducing air, surface, and subsurface units, new creatures, and spells. *Warcraft II: Beyond the Dark Portal* is no exception to this guessing game. Each encounter offers a new puzzle to solve or challenge to meet. One scenario consists of a straight-out build-and-conquer challenge while the next may require a degree of stealth as you attempt to liberate your captured Peasants.

Warcraft appeals to players from many walks and varying levels of gaming life. Many are tried-and-true fantasy gamers who tired, perhaps, of the same old adventure in the same old dungeons. *Warcraft*'s Mages, Death Knights, Dragons, and others, give them new ways to employ familiar beings.

Surprisingly, many of the *Warcraft* hard core are dyed-in-the-wool strategy and war gamers. The game's nerve-wracking choices attract the strategic types. *What do I build next? A Lumber Mill will let me upgrade my Scout Towers, but I really ought to start the Barracks.* War gamers appreciate the tactics of pseudo-medieval battle. It's amazing how well sound combined-arms strategies work in *Warcraft*. The plethora of units offers the classic paper-covers-rock-crushes-scissors-cuts-paper. Ballistas can devastate buildings and exposed troopers, yet a Ballista is dead meat if a Grunt gets close enough to lay his axe on one. An Ogre-Mage Runes spell coupled with a Catapult bombardment can even replicate the deadly mine-and-shrapnel-riddled no-man's-land of World War I.

Yet all this may truly be a sidebar to what is one of the strongest points of the game—head-to-head play. Let's face it. The computer is pretty dumb. Matching wits in real time evens the odds somewhat (I know I can't mouse my men as quickly as the computer). However, *we* learn from our mistakes; the computer doesn't. Thankfully, when we tire of bashing the motherboard, tougher adversaries wait in cyberland.

I reviewed the original *Warcraft* for Prodigy's "Computer Gaming World" section and asked Blizzard what they liked about the game. Bill Roper's response was the perfect testament to the excitement of head-to-head play: "The real-time format of *Warcraft* makes for some of the most gut-wrenching white knuckled hair-pulling one-on-one competition we've engaged in for quite some time." Amen.

The computer gives you breathers, falls for simple traps, and fails to efficiently utilize its forces; most humans won't offer such easy prey. It's the unpredictable tension of confronting another sentient being that offers an addictive challenge.

Nevertheless, you can attribute *Warcraft*'s success to one overarching quality. No, not the graphics, the clever voice-overs, or nifty magic spells. And despite all Blizzard's work it's not the scenarios, maps, or the plethora of units. Gamers love *Warcraft* for one reason: It's fun.

Recently a gamer called Blizzard's technical support line. It was after hours and the line was set to tape questions for answering the next day. The gamer, however, believed he was on hold and stayed on the line. After a moment his wife picked up an extension and, peeved, reminded her husband he'd promised to turn off the game long ago. The husband offered the age-old "Yes, Dear" mantra of the henpecked spouse. The wife's ensuing tirade ended with a quote that describes the extent of *Warcraft*'s pull better than I ever could:

"You know," she shrieked, "that game is why we never have sex."

Using the Book

Chapter 1 is kind of like the Sears and Roebuck catalogue of playing *Warcraft II: Beyond the Dark Portal*. In it, I include general tips that apply throughout the game. Chapters 2 and 3 provide nuts-and-bolts walkthroughs of the Great Alliance and Orc missions. If a particular scenario is kicking your tail, this is the place to go. The tips tell you where you are, where the bad guy is, what you have to do to win, and how to do it. Finally, we include various tables and cheats in the appendix for a further advantage. I highly recommend using the "On-screen" cheat. The computer does.

Chapter One

Beating the System

Basic Strategies for Winning Warcraft II

Okay, okay, so you're ready to jump right in. Don't let me stop you. Just page back to the scenario that's kicking your tail and start reading. I guarantee you'll beat the computer next time around.

But maybe you're the kind of Orc or pathetic Human (as the case may be) who wants to be the best cybergeneral in the history of Azeroth.

If so, read on.

There's more to winning *Warcraft II: Beyond the Dark Portal* than learning where the mines are. Blizzard took the time to create units with complex interactions. Understanding the general strategies that take advantage of this complex system is critical to winning, whether you face the CPU or your buddy down the road.

The Artillery Barrage

Frequently the enemy must approach your village through a narrow passage. Setting two or three Catapults or Ballistas to bombard the area of approach will seriously weaken, if not kill, approaching bad guys. Plus, they'll work on "autopilot" so you can focus your attention elsewhere.

The Wall of Steel

Placing a couple of Guard and Cannon Towers in a narrow passage can shut it down quick (place the Cannon behind the Guard Towers because of their range advantage). This is most effective when used with the artillery barrage, deadly when coupled with the working party described below, and impregnable with a couple of Grunts or Footmen at the base.

The Wooden Band-Aid

The only problem with the foregoing is the enemy—they can be so damned inconsiderate! They'll do their level best to take out the Towers. If the going gets dicey, detail two or three Peons/Peasants to repair each Tower. As long as they stay on the opposite side of the attack the computer won't bother them. The Towers will stand up to brutal punishment because the workers repair them as fast as they're damaged. If you place the Towers so each can cover the others' bases, they can pick off any attackers hacking at their Tower counterparts. Please note that this will not work against Catapults and Ballistas.

Figure 1.1 *The cats lay down some steel.*

Lumber Mills as Town Halls

In many scenarios, you must erect the Town Hall or Great Hall at some distance from the nearest lumber. Be not dismayed: Lumber may also be dropped at Lumber Mills. To accumulate it faster, merely build a Lumber Mill near the woods.

Death Knights as Recruiters

This is too cool. When the computer runs out of gold it sends Peasants to the closest active mine—even if *you* own it. Place a three-Grunts, one-Death-Knight reception committee at the mine in question. As Peasants arrive, the Grunts kill them and the Knight raises them from the dead—effectively recruiting them into the Orcish Horde. Like I said—too cool.

Strength in Numbers

Subtle tactics rarely work in *Warcraft II*. Don't be bashful about ganging up on the enemy. It's not like he won't do it to you. There's a saying among military explosives experts: "If 10 pounds of C4 will do the job, 20 will do it twice as well." Ditto for *Beyond the Dark Portal* (or any in the *Warcraft* series). Mobs of Grunts or Footmen backed up by Axethrowers or Archers can devastate almost anything in their path. The game allows you to group together up to nine units. It's usually a darned good idea. I group eight, then right-click on a ninth, ordering the group to follow him (or it). Make this "ninth" a distinct unit if you can. For example, place an Ogre in charge of a group of fully upgraded Grunts and Axethrowers.

Figure 1.2 *An Ogre-led assault force*

The Tripwire Defense

Late in the Iran/Iraq war of the 1980s, Iraq implemented a defensive tactic made famous by Germany in W.W.II. The Iraqis, unable to match the Iranian's manpower, were hard put to defend the entire length of their line. Instead, Saddam's boys decided to lightly garrison their front and hold strong-armored formations in reserve to counterattack Iranian incursions. When the Iranians attacked, the light forces defending the front line functioned as a tripwire, notifying the rear echelons of the crises and delaying the attackers until reserve units could be brought to bear.

The same holds true for *Warcraft II* (without Iraqi T-72 tanks, that is). Several *Dark Portal* missions require a 360-village defense with limited resources. Try placing a light outer ring of Guard Towers and Footmen/Grunt types with a strong counterattack force (Ogres and the like) in the center of the village. When the enemy hits the outer ring, counterattack and crush them with the Ogres. Of course, if the bad guys attack two places at once, you're screwed. I've said it before: those bad guys can be *so* inconsiderate.

The Offensive Defense

You'll never win a *Dark Portal* scenario by defending a base. Players often overlook this obvious fact. If constant attacks threaten to overwhelm your encampment, it's time either to start over or to take the offense. Frequently, the only way to get the computer off your back is to get on *its* back. Form a reserve and start hitting one of the computer's villages. This usually forces the motherboard to concentrate its resources on defense, removing some of the pressure from you.

The Defensive Offense

Try this neat trick when attacking. Stop your formation just out of enemy range. Place Footmen/Grunts in front, Archers/Axethrowers immediately behind. Now bombard, cast a spell on, or send someone to taunt the opposing line. When the enemy reacts by charging the threat to their front, they will march into the teeth of your prepared defenses.

The Red Beast Burger

You didn't know these guys were good for something besides blocking construction and emitting excellent screams when slaughtered, did you? Well, they are. If a Death Knight utilizing Death Coil kills a Red Beast, he gains three health points. Not a big deal, but in some scenarios—"The Slayer of The Shadowmoon," for instance—this may be what keeps these creepy guys creeping.

Combat Farm Houses

Maybe I'm stretching it here. Nevertheless, Warcraft buildings *can* assist you in defending your village. Let's say the Alliance are streaming into your settlement from two directions. One of these avenues of approach is through a narrow valley bordered by woods and rocks. Let's say the valley is about as wide as a Pig Farm. Are you starting to get the picture? Building a Pig Farm in the valley blocks the Men, and their Elf cousins, from gaining easy access to the village. This is great used in conjunction with the tripwire defense.

Figure 1.3 *Dining at the Beast Burger Inn*

What's Up with Those Upgrades, Anyway?

After you buy and research an upgrade, it affects *all* units—those currently in play as well as future purchases. Subsequently destroying the building used for the improvement (for example, Elven Lumber Mill, Blacksmith) does *not* cancel the upgrade.

What's Up With All This Basic, Piercing, and Effective Damage Stuff?

Glad you asked. This is how combat works in *Warcraft II*: To get the attacker's Effective Damage (what is actually applied to the defender each time the attacker strikes), a defender's Armor rating is subtracted from the attacker's Basic rating Damage (this value can never be less than zero) and then Piercing Damage is applied (Piercing is unaffected by Armor). After this is figured, there is a random chance that only half the damage will be inflicted (it's all or half). For example: Ogre (Basic Damage eight, Piercing Damage four) attacks an Alliance Footman (Armor two). The Ogre's Effective Damage would be his Basic Damage (eight) minus the Footman's Armor (two), plus the Ogre's Piercing Damage (four).

$$8 - 2 + 4 = 10$$

The Ogre's Effective Damage when attacking the Footman equals ten (with the exception of the random "half damage" calculation cutting the attack to five). So Effective Damage is five or ten.

You Can Never Have Too Much Money . . . Or Can You?

The two rules of thumb when it comes to money are: If you don't have enough, you'll probably lose, and if you have too much, you'll probably lose. On one hand, you need a constant cash flow to finance builds, upgrades, and training. That's why training Peons/Peasants should be on the top of your scenario "to do" list. On the other hand, too much money is a sure sign you're not building, upgrading, or training quickly enough. Look at the situation. Are you waiting on construction? Then assign more workers to repair each building. Always a Footman short? Then build a couple more Barracks and train two or three at once. The perfect situation is enough cash to do what you want but not much more.

HERE LIES
ANDUIN
LOTHAR
· · ·
LION OF
AZEROTH

METZEN · 96

Chapter Two

The Alliance

. . . of Dwarves, Elves, and Men

Mission One
Alleria's Journey

Lord Khadgar, Keeper of the Eternal Watch, and master of the mystic Citadel of Nethergarde, has sensed a dark power gathering around the remnants of the rift that lies within the Black Morass. He believes that a new Orcish invasion is imminent, and has urged the Alliance to act. The Elven Ranger Alleria, and a small band of her elite guard, have been sent as escorts so that you may gather reinforcements to counter this threat.

Your travels to the Castle of New Stormwind will lead you across the paths of both the Paladin, Turalyon, and a mercenary captain known as Danath. Engage their aid during your journey, as their leadership may be needed by the Alliance in the dark days ahead.

Marching Orders

- ✖ **Objectives:** Find Turalyon. Find Danath. Bring the Heroes Alleria, Turalyon and Danath to the Circle of Power at New Stormwind.

- ✖ **Starting Location:** Southeast corner.

- ✖ **Enemy Location:** Distributed in small clusters.

- ✖ **Resources:** One Lumber Mill in the lower center of map.

Courtesy Calls

Gather your band and move north along the eastern map border. Reverse a short distance past the first intersection and dispatch three Knights to destroy the trailing Catapult.

✠ ✠ ✠ ✠ ✠ ✠

TIP *The Knights move too fast for the Catapult to target. It will track and slaughter slower units. If you don't go far enough beyond the fork, the Catapult will be supported by a Grunt and a Troll stationed just beyond the intersection.*

✠ ✠ ✠

Continue north and recruit the Ballista. March to the river village and liberate all you find there. Return with your entourage to the previously passed clearing. Walk southwest to an intersection bordered by mountains. Follow the foothills, kill the Ogres, stop at the pass, and array your troops in a defensive formation.

Be careful. Some greenskins, supported by a Catapult, wait on the other side.

Have your Knights charge the gap and draw the Cat's fire. The accompanying Grunts should follow the horsemen onto your troops' waiting swords. Once you've massacred the Orcs you can make kindling of the Cat.

After the battle for the pass, move northeast to the Lumber Mill and put the Peasants to work. You'll find a new recruit just north to assist them. Keep your guard up; powerful Orc forces—including a Juggernaught—roam the area. Destroy the greenskin infantry; then sink the Juggernaught. If you can, try to hole the Transport as well, although it will leave the scene quickly.

Figure 2.1 *The Alliance troop waits at the pass.*

✠ ✠ ✠ ✠ ✠ ✠

TIP *Use the Knights to draw the Juggernaught's fire.
Move your Ballista into range and let loose. You'll
need Archers to support the Ballista, otherwise the
Jug might get a shot off that could cause a major owie
for the Archers. If you feel exceptionally cunning,
have the Knights exit from the Jug's view after draw-
ing its fire. The Juggernaught will then bombard the
closest farm while you sink the imperceptive behe-
moth.*

✠ ✠ ✠

Return to the Gap. You can rescue Danath two ways:

- **Choice A:** The safest approach is to continue following the eastern ridge until the forest thins. When you spot a farmhouse on the wood's far side, use the Peasants to deforest the area and move through the hole. Next to the abode waits Danath. This is boring, but necessary if you've lost most of your troops.

- **Choice B:** From the gap in the mountains follow the western path. You'll meet a Death Knight who'll cast Whirlwind on your troops and then run north—the cowardly scum. Pursue, overtake, and slay the Death Knight and his Undead cronies. Follow the southern path. Danath waits a short way down this trail.

METZEN - 95

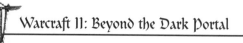
After recruiting Danath, send your military units back to the Shipyard and Foundry settlement. Keep the Peasants harvesting lumber. Build a Transport and upgrade the arrows.

Before boarding the waiting Transport, creep west along the river to ambush the Troll Destroyer waiting there. The Ballista does a good job on this fellow. Now, cross the river, journey west, kill some Undead, and head north up their path. You'll find Turalyon at the Church. Say a prayer, ugrade your Knights, reboard the ferry, and sail west. Unload on the north bank west of the mountains. After you chop up the Undead guards, use your Ballista to take out the Guard Towers.

Figure 2.2 *The Ballista's turn the Tower to rubble.*

✗ ✗ ✗ ✗ ✗ ✗

TIP *Remember: Order the Ballista to engage the Guard Towers while still out of range. The Ballista will stop at its maximum range (two "squares" longer than the Guard Towers') and fire with impunity.*

✗ ✗ ✗

Move northwest, annihilate remaining enemy forces, run your heroes through the Circle of Power and *voila!*—we have a winner!

Mission Two
The Battle for Nethergarde

A great host of Orcs have reconstructed the Dark Portal and now lay siege to the Citadel of Nethergarde. The Horde still maintain their hold over the great winged dragons of Azeroth. A faction of these creatures, seeming to have grown to crave the taste of battle, have become willing allies with the Orcs under the leadership of a great Black Dragon known only as Deathwing.

Danath has been asked to raise an army from New Stormwind to relieve the beleaguered forces at Nethergarde and drive the Horde back towards the Portal. You must lead the forces of Azeroth in an attempt to break the vanguard of the invading Horde, for unless their assault is stopped, they will gain dominion over the Black Morass.

Marching Orders

- ✠ **Objectives:** Destroy all enemy forces. Danath must survive.

- ✠ **Starting Location:** Southwest corner.

- ✠ **Enemy Location:** Shadowmoon clan—center; Warsong clan—northwest corner; Laughing Skull clan—southeast corner.

- ✠ **Resources:** Six Gold Mines—northwest, southeast (two), northeast corner, northeast-center, west-center.

Fight the Good Fight

Trudge northeast, scouting ahead with the Gnomish Flying Machine and brushing aside the pitiful Orc warriors in your path. Set up camp near the Mine, constructing a Town Hall and Lumber Mill. Watch your back! An Ogrish trio creeps up the trail. After butchering the Ogres, head north and scout out a river crossing. Don't cross right away—the far bank boasts some serious firepower.

Back at the Nethergarde ranch, things look pretty green. Don't sweat it. Not much can be done to prevent the township's capture. Instead, focus your attention on the upcoming battle for the river crossing.

Move your Ballista to the stream and engage the southern Guard Tower. Move Knights, one at a time, over the water and gal-

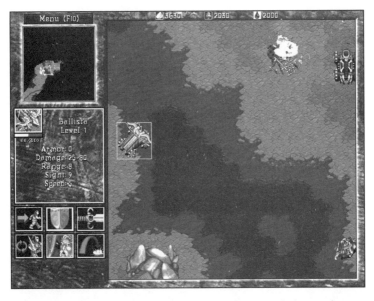

Figure 2.3 Placement of units when attacking the crossing

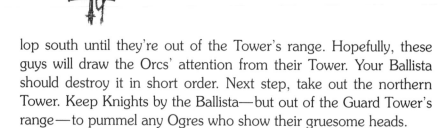
lop south until they're out of the Tower's range. Hopefully, these guys will draw the Orcs' attention from their Tower. Your Ballista should destroy it in short order. Next step, take out the northern Tower. Keep Knights by the Ballista—but out of the Guard Tower's range—to pummel any Ogres who show their gruesome heads.

On the economic front, expand your village and commence liberating Nethergarde. Send a squad of units to the city's south wall. Place your Footmen and Archers in a good defensive formation just inside the east gate. Order them to stand and bring up a Ballista to pound the Orc barracks.

The red-eyes will reply piecemeal, presenting little more than mobile targets to the Alliance veterans. Once you've neutralized their military, slaughter the Peons and have the Peasants construct a Cannon Tower (it will immediately open up on all in sight).

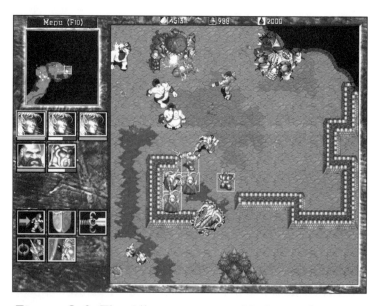

Figure 2.4 *The Alliance reenters Nethergarde.*

Don't forget your own town. The nothing-if-not-persistent greenskins will mount numerous small-scale raids. One note: An ounce of preventive Guard Tower construction is better than a pound of rebuilding after a couple of Dragon fly-bys. Keep Danath in the center of your village from now on. You don't need him and losing him means another saved game down the drain.

Focus most of your efforts on economics during the mid- to late game. Build a second Town Hall in Nethergarde and a third northeast of it. Research and purchase all the upgrades you can afford.

Once the research is complete and you're churning out full-up Ballistas, Footmen, and Paladins, take two Ballistas, a couple of Paladins, a few Footmen, and head northwest. You'll see a gap in the mountains overlooked by two Guard Towers. Attack with the Ballistas. A high-level Grunt or Troll will seek revenge and you can axe him with your Knights. Be careful to spring the ambush outside the Towers' range. Once you've weeded out the Orcish foot soldiers, let your Ballistas blast away.

Having silenced the Towers, you're free to sack the Orc village. Let the Ballistas handle any remaining Towers while your troops destroy the buildings. You'll find no enemy soldiers past the mountain gap.

After leveling the northwest village, send a similar force to the southeastern Orc encampment. This village is even more lightly defended than the last. Again, use your Ballista to destroy the Towers. There shouldn't be more than one or two other Orc warriors. Build a couple of Cannon Towers, destroy everything in sight, and you'll know victory.

Mission Three

Once More Unto the Breach

Having broken the momentum of the Horde offensive at Nethergarde, the time is ripe for a decisive counterattack. The High Command agrees that a strong assault upon the fortress that the Orcs have raised near the Dark Portal may well end the conflict before it has rightly begun.

The Arch-Wizard Khadgar, however, believes that the Orcish Hordes may not be here for the sake of mere conquest. He believes that if the Portal can be captured and not destroyed, he can uncover the purpose for the Horde's present invasion into Azeroth.

Marching Orders

- ✠ **Objectives:** Destroy all strongholds and fortresses. Turalyon must reach the Dark Portal alive.

- ✠ **Starting Location:** Southwest-center.

- ✠ **Enemy Location:** Bleeding Hollow clan—southeast corner; Warsong clan—center, midwest; Thunderlord clan—north-center, upper islands.

- ✠ **Resources:** Five Gold Mines—mid-north, center, east-center, southwest, southeast. Four Oil splotches: west-center, east-center, south-center, southeast.

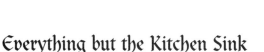

Everything but the Kitchen Sink

First off, put those Peasants to work. Next, upgrade your Scout Towers to Guard status. Third, stand by for incoming rounds. A small force of Ogre-lead greenskins attacks. Position your Footmen across the gateway with a "Stand" order. Have your Archers back them up with the Ballista. These units, in addition to your Guard Towers, will make quick work of these bad guys.

Continue training Peasants and a couple more Footmen, and begin funding research and upgrades. Watch your food supply and build Farms as you need them.

Send your Knights, a Peasant, Turalyon, the Ballista, and two Footmen over the river crossing. March northwest until you come to a couple of Orcish Towers under construction. Destroy them. Proceed to the gap in the mountains and attack the Guard Tower. Watch out for counterattacks from Orcs who recently ferried across the river.

Once the Ballista has collapsed the Tower, turn its awesome arrows on the Temple to the north. Have the other soldiers destroy the Lumber Mill while the Peasant builds a Town Hall near the mine. Leave at least one unit outside the mountain pass to guard against Orc landings.

Pump up the economy with more Peasants gathering lumber and gold. Use the money to finish outfitting your army and construct a solid defense for the second village, which will receive the brunt of the Orc attacks. This defense should include at least four Guard Towers and several Archers to meet the inevitable Dragon attacks. Meantime, upgrade your Keep in the main village to Castle, then build a Church, Gryphon Aviary, and Mage Hall.

Once your production is going nicely and you can fight off the incessant raids, prepare for your assault on the large concentration of Orcs in the southeast corner.

Figure 2.5 *A wall of arrows and steel, the human defense of the second village*

You'll want two Ballistas, two Gryphons, two Paladins, four Rangers, four Footmen, and a pair of Mages. After crossing the stream just north of your main village, head for the gap in the mountains. This is the entrance to the first Orc settlement. Place the Gryphons, the Archers, a Footman, a Paladin, and a Mage as backup in a defensive perimeter west-northwest of your position. They'll defend your backside from Dragons or a roving band of Orc nasties.

Assault the village with the standard fire-the-Ballista-and-draw-them-out-to-their-death tactic. Keep a close rein on your ambushers, or they'll follow retreating units through the gap and become the ambushees. Keep your Mage and Paladin on hand to counter the inevitable Death Knight.

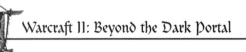

As you subdue the village, kill off Peons whenever possible. These seemingly innocent Orcs repair buildings you want to destroy and harvest resources that could be yours. With the Towers destroyed, it's safe to bring Peasants in to erect a Town Hall. When the Hall is complete, build a couple of Towers and a Barracks to ward off those irksome Dragons.

Dive into an aggressive shipbuilding program and explore the rest of the map with the Gnomish Flying Machine. A river cuts the map in half. In the center you'll see an island shaped like a smile, another, frown-like, island above it, and a small, circular island in the middle where the Portal stands.

Conquer the southern island first. Use Ballistas to hit the enemy Oil Platforms and replace them with your own. The Cannon Towers along much of the Orc shoreline make good target practice for the Gryphon Riders and Mages. Build a couple of Battleships to destroy Refineries, Shipyards, and the occasional Foundry. Once the sea lanes are clear, load a Transport with Ballistas and ground troops. Hit the beach! Resistance is usually light. Once the island is secure, build a Barracks.

If the Orcs are being aggressive, however, they'll build throngs of Dragons, Juggernaughts, and Destroyers. Use Guard Towers and Destroyers to kill the Dragons. Have decoys lure the Dragons to the friendly Guard Towers—the winged lizards don't seem to have a sense of self-preservation. Use Ballistas and Gryphons against the greenskin Juggernaughts.

Next in line is the center island. You'll need at least two Ballistas and a pair of Paladins for the job. Exorcise the Death Knights using the Paladins and use the Ballista to take down the northern Guard Towers. Collapse the walls surrounding the Circle of Power and run Turalyon through it.

Figure 2.6 *The Alliance takes up positions on the center isle.*

Finally, destroy the fortress on the northern island—*way* easier said than done. The island often contains numerous Catapults, Death Knights, and Ogres. Land on an edge of the island, behind the forests. This limits the Orcs' avenues of approach to the coastline. Use your ships to hit any units moving down the coast. Gradually move your forces up the coast toward the center. If Dragons are out, build Towers. At this point you outproduce the Orc commander, so he should run out of units far faster than you. Take your time, wear him down, and victory will be yours.

Mission Four

Beyond the Dark Portal

Elven scouts bring chilling news from Azeroth. A tearing of shadows heralded the arrival of the mighty Orc Shaman Ner'zhul and his guard of Death Knights within the Royal Library of New Stormwind. Unleashing their black magiks, they slaughtered all who opposed them and then fled into the night with their prize — The Book of Medivh.

This serves to confirm what Khadgar has gleaned from the Battle of Nethergarde. He is convinced that the Horde is attempting to learn how the great sorcerer opened the rift between our world and that of the Horde known in the Book of Medivh only as Draenor.

With countless domains to plunder, the Horde would become an unstoppable power. The High Command believes that our only recourse is to venture through the Portal — both to reclaim the Book of Medivh and to ensure that the Horde can never again threaten Azeroth.

Marching Orders

- **Objectives:** Erect a Castle to protect lands near the Portal. Destroy all enemy forces.

- **Starting Location:** Center of map.

- **Enemy Location:** Shattered Hand clan — south-center; Warsong clan — west-center; Shadowmoon clan — northeast; Laughing Skull clan — scattered about.

※ Resources: Four Gold Mines—two south, one west-center, one northeast.

Kickin' Green Butt

Your first objective is the Shattered Hand village. Use the Gnomish Flying Machine to scout the southern area for possible ambushes while your Gryphon Rider eliminates the Cannon Towers guarding the Portal's eastern passes. You should be able to capture this village rather easily. Have one of your Peasants begin building a Town Hall midway between the two Gold Mines in the area. Have the others build plenty of Farms and a Barracks.

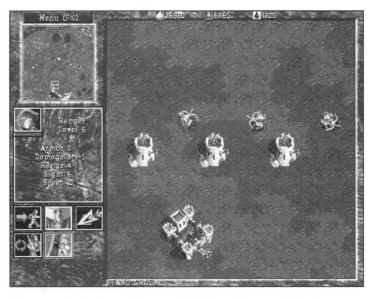

Figure 2.7 *An effective AD (Anti-Dragon) defensive line*

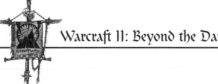
The other clans will waste no time badgering your new settlement. Move most of your troops to cover the western approaches, but keep several Archers and your Gryphon Rider to the northeast to protect against Dragon attacks.

As soon as possible, build a string of Guard Towers north of your town and position Archers between each. Three or four Towers will do the trick.

As your settlement grows, form a hammer to smash the greenskins.

Your next target is the Warsong clan to the northwest. Divide your force and attack through the two southern passes. Lead with Ballistas, covering them with your foot soldiers and Archers. Take out the Towers first. This fight can be tough, so be sure to have reserves ready. After leveling the village, build a Town Hall and start collecting coin. Oh—a small garrison might be a good idea, too. Orcs have a sneaky habit of rebuilding their villages after the destroying armies leave.

The last city is a pretty tough nut to crack. Train two armies. Position one at north-center of the map and the other east-center.

Figure 2.8 *Gryphons raid the Dragon Roosts.*

Slowly advance within Ballista range of the Towers and eliminate them. Gryphon Riders also work well against Cannon Towers (or just about anything, for that matter). As the Orcs pour forth to defend their village, bring up the troops. Once you've thinned the ranks of green, use your Ballistas and Gryphons to take out the Dragon roosts, severely throttling the Orcish air support.

The rest of the battle is just sacking the village.

Mission Five

The Shadowed Seas

*Having fortified your position on the Hellfire penin-
sula where the Portal is located, the time has come to
establish a fleet to attack the surrounding clans. The
Orcish shipyards of Zeth'kur lie nearby, and for our
plans to progress you must destroy them and the ships
of war that are stationed there.*

*While the Horde has been stunned by the ferocity
of your attack, our presence here has driven the clans
to new heights of fury. You will be unable to maintain
this foothold for long against their numbers, so your
victories must be daring and swift.*

METZEN · 95

Marching Orders

- ✠ **Objectives:** Build three Shipyards. Destroy the Orcish
  Shipyards of Zeth'kur.

- ✠ **Starting Location:** Northwest corner of map.

- ✠ **Enemy Location:** Bonechewer clan—northwest; Bleeding
  Hollow clan—center; Thunderlord clan—southwest; Laughing Skull clan—southeast.

- ✠ **Resources:** Eight Gold Mines—four on the north side of
  the sea located northwest, north-center, center and northeast; two on the southwestern islands; one south-center; one
  southeast. Six Oil patches—west-center, center, east-center,
  south-center, southwest and southeast.

Sweeping the Seas

A straightforward scenario, just remember the objectives and stick to them. Start by assaulting the Bonechewer village south of your starting position. The Bonechewers are a weak clan and present little resistance. Immediately begin building a base of operations on the ruins of the Bone-head settlement. Position your forces to defend against attacks from the east.

Pump up your army; then send out a reconnaissance in force. You may want to leave the Ballistas behind in case a quick retreat is necessary. Once you discover the Bleeding Hollow clan (to the east), build up your forces and make a direct assault. They're closely allied with the Laughing Skulls to the south, so prepare for seaborne reinforcements. Raze the village, build a Town Hall and commence digging for gold.

Scout the remainder of the north shore, using Knights. Next you must construct Shipyards, Oil Tankers, five Destroyers (to hunt drilling sites), a Gnomish Inventor, and a Foundry.

Fabricate an undersea armada to use against the Thunderlord clan's navy. These greenskins, from islands in the map's southwestern quadrant, own an impressive force of Juggernauts and Destroyers—impressive against *surface* combatants, that is. Little more than targets for Gnomish Submarines. While this battle rages, build Battleships to bombard the Orc coastal Cannon Towers.

Don't lose sight of the undersea war. The Thunderlords get plenty tricky, employing Death Knights to cast Whirlwind spells powerful enough to sink your Subs. Your newly constructed Battleships can lend a hand, bombarding the Coastal Towers and Death Knights who wait on the shore to cast their evil spells of destruction.

From now on, this is an engagement for Admirals. Pound the Orcs with your navy while the Alliance's army guards the northern shore. Once you've destroyed the Thunderlord navy and Shipyards,

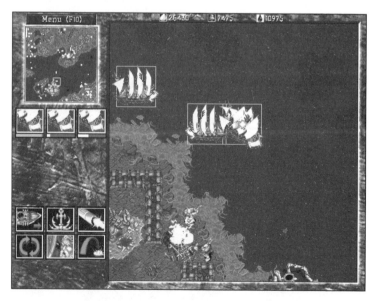

Figure 2.9 *Shore bombardment*

Figure 2.10 The southern isle

move east to take out the Laughing Skulls. Their navy is smaller than the Thunderlords', but their coastal defenses, studded with Catapults, can be wicked. It's possible to win the battle without Transports, but you may want to land a force of Marines to assist in the Laughing Skulls' destruction. Remember, you need not destroy all enemy forces, only their Shipyards.

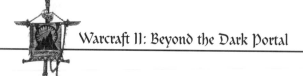

Mission Six

The Fall of Auchindouin

Kurdran—Gryphon Rider of Northeron—has returned from his patrol with vital news. He has located the hidden Fortress of Auchindoun and the battlements that serve as stronghold to The Bleeding Hollow clan. Alleria's Rangers also report that they have seen a massive force moving towards the North, and suspect that these troops are staging for another attack upon Azeroth.

Although the Orcish army is too large for your forces to battle alone, you may be able to launch a raid against Auchindoun. Should your strike succeed, you would force their army to retreat—or be cut off and destroyed.

Raze the Fortress of Auchindoun and retreat before their forces can rally against you.

Marching Orders

- ✠ **Objectives:** Destroy Auchindoun. Return the Heroes Turalyon and Danath to the Circle of Power.

- ✠ **Starting Location:** Northeast corner

- ✠ **Enemy Location:** Bonechewer clan—northwest; Warsong clan—east-center; Bleeding Hollow clan—southwest; Shadowmoon clan—south-center.

Resources: Six Gold Mines—three along the eastern map edge in the north, center and south; one northwest, one southwest; one south-center. Four Oil patches—all in the center.

From the Jaws of Defeat

This scenario is difficult even *with* this guide. If you fail to stick to the objectives, the last thing you'll see will be the business end of an Orc battleax. First off, establish a base. Use your Gnomish Flying Machines to scout the land mass directly south of your starting position. Ferry your forces across the water, landing just south of the village.

At this point, you have two options. The best is to capture the Warsong village. This is arduous duty, but it's better for the Alliance in the long run. Nevertheless, if you desire, you may base near the Gold Mine in the east-central edge of the map and defeat the Warsongs after you build up your forces. The Warsongs won't just sit and wait for your attack, however. Count on these dental-hygiene-challenged dudes doing all they can to disrupt your plans for economic force enhancement.

If you decide to take the village at the start, position your Destroyers and Battleships along the shore, near the pass leading to the village. Then move your Ballistas forward to engage one of the Towers. When the Orcs counterattack, withdraw your Ballistas toward your ships and remaining soldiers. Repeat this drill several times, eliminating most of this Orcish Horde. Now you can concentrate on destroying the Towers and sacking the village.

This is a great spot to build your base. You'll find a prolific Gold Mine and an Oil patch nearby. The mountains provide natural protection from land attack.

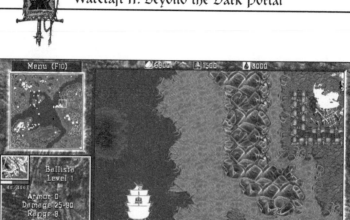

Figure 2.11 *Lure enemy units from the Towers into range of your naval guns.*

Right off, build Guard Towers to protect against Shawdowmoon Dragon raids. The Towers also come in handy against the amphibious incursions of the Bonechewer clan. Archers with Ranger training and upgraded arrows help round out your defenses.

Beef up your forces and eventually upgrade your Town Hall to a Castle. Three or four Gryphon Riders are excellent not only for defending your base, but for attacking enemy ships and Cannon Towers. Hammer out a few Submarines to help sink enemy ships, as well.

As in all things, stick to your guns. Protect Turalyon and Danath and don't worry about much aside from the destruction of Auchindoun. Once your force is large enough to fill four Transports, send a force of Gryphon Riders south to take out any remaining Bleeding Hollow Cannon Towers.

Bring along a few Battleships for shore bombardment.

The fight for Auchindoun will be bloody and require constant attention. Ignore attacks on your home base—that distraction could cost you the battle. The homeboy Archers and Guard Towers should be sufficient, in any case. Leave Turalyon and Danath at the base with a small bodyguard. As soon as you destroy the last Bleeding Hollow unit in Auchindoun, rush them across to the Circle of Power and victory will be yours.

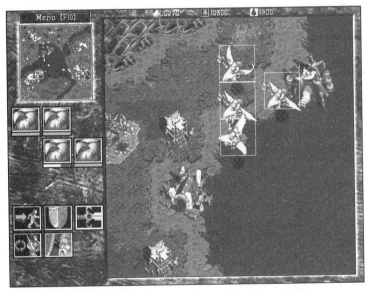

Figure 2.12 *Use Gryphon Riders to eliminate Cannon Towers.*

Mission Seven

Deathwing

The arcane powers that surround the blazing ruins of Auchindoun have made urgent the summoning of Khadgar to the dark lands of the Orcs. The destruction of the Bleeding Hollow clan was not without great price, however, for both Kurdran and his mount Sky'ree were captured by the Horde.

While examining the remains of the great Fortress, the Arch-Wizard has learned not only the location of the Book of Medivh, but also that another artifact is needed for Ner'zhul's plans to reach fruition—the Skull of Gul'dan. Khadgar believes it will be possible to destroy the Portal and permanently seal the rift created by Medivh if he can acquire these artifacts.

A great mountain isle lies to the northeast, atop which the Black Dragon Deathwing dwells. The Skull of Gul'dan lies within his lair. Alleria and Khadgar have agreed to aid you in stealing away the Skull and—if possible—destroy the great Dragon. It is rumored that Orcish tribes live on this island and offer captives from the Great War as sacrifices to Deathwing. If you can rescue them, they may know of some weakness in the creature . . .

Marching Orders

- ✠ **Objectives:** Destroy Deathwing and his lair. Khadgar, Alleria and Kurdan must survive.

- ✠ **Starting Location:** Southwest corner of the map.

✖ **Enemy Location:** Bonechewer clan—southeast corner; Shattered Hand clan—northwest quadrant; Warsongclan—northeast quadrant; Deathwing and his lair—east of center.

✖ **Resources:** Three Gold Mines—southeast, northwest and mideast. Two Oil patches—south-center and southeast corner.

Lizards to Go

This battle allows you to get up-close and personal with your charge, since what you start with is all you get. Warm up by destroying the Bonechewer village east of your starting position. Here's how: Load your troops in the Transport and head for the village, Destroyers in the lead. Have the Elven ships bombard the shore while the troops disembark. This engagement will go quickly, but be careful not to lose anyone. Don't let your wounded die—use your Paladins to heal them.

After you free the captives, have the Peasants build a Town Hall, several Farms, a Lumber Mill, Oil Refinery, and Shipyard. Divide your forces to protect the Transports and village from Dragon attacks. Have the Shipyard crank out a few Tankers and all the Destroyers your coin will allow. While you expand your navy, the Gnomish Flying Machine can scout the map to locate other captives.

Once the Gold Mine collapses, load up your troops and set sail for the northwestern map edge. You'll pass the western shore of Shattered Hand Island. Don't trade shots with the locals. Their Giant Turtles wait beneath the surface to sink your forces. Above all, protect the Transports.

After passing by the island, head east and land your troops. Use the Destroyers to exterminate the red-eyes' nasty welcoming committee. Once your troops are ashore, advance east to rescue the captured Paladin and his compatriots. Take care: Although resistance is light, you can't afford to lose a single sword.

✠ ✠ ✠ ✠ ✠ ✠

TIP *After each engagement, heal the wounded and give the magic folk time to regain their power. Don't recklessly expose Khadgar or Alleria. If either die, you lose the battle. Save your game often, especially right before an attack.*

✠ ✠ ✠

Two Cannon Towers and several Undead guard the entrance to the final POW camp. First, lure the Undead outside the Towers and destroy them. Then send Khadgar to unleash a Blizzard on the

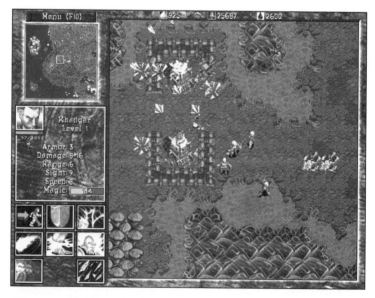

Figure 2.13 *A little magic in the air—Use Blizzard to take out Towers.*

Figure 2.14 *The trap springs on Deathwing*

Towers. If the first spell doesn't crumble them both, wait until Khadgar's power is recharged and let the ice fall once again. After destroying the Towers, advance cautiously, taking out the remaining Undead and Catapult.

The mountains southeast of this final POW camp harbor Deathwing and his lair. Kurdran is the only figure capable of reaching it, but he can't defeat this powerful Dragon alone. Position your Archers in a line near the pass leading to the lair. Keep the Paladins nearby to heal their wounds. Once this trap is ready, have Kurdran attack Deathwing. As soon as the Dragon responds, withdraw Kurdran through the line of Archers. When Deathwing comes in range, have Khadgar cast a "Slow" spell on the Dragon. This gives your Archers time to defeat this great menace. Afterward, send Kurdran in to destroy the lair.

Mission Eight
Coast of Bones

By seeking the artifacts you need to seal the rift, you've given the Horde time to mount a strike against you. A great Orcish armada threatens your captured coasts, and Alliance armies are pressed hard on many fronts.

Your only chance for victory lies in obtaining the Book of Medivh. All knowledge of the Portal rests in the keeping of Ner'zhul and his Order of Death Knights at the Fortress of Shadowmoon. You must storm and raze the Strongholds that guard the coastline of his lands so you may bring your forces to bear and isolate and destroy his cursed sanctuary.

Marching Orders

- ✠ **Objective:** Destroy all enemy forces.

- ✠ **Starting Location:** Central northern map edge.

- ✠ **Enemy Location:** Shattered Hand clan—northwest; Thunderlord clan—southwest; Laughing Skull clan—southeast.

- ✠ **Resources:** Five Gold Mines—southwest, center, southeast and two northwest. Four Oil patches—west-center, southeast corner, and two center.

Wipe 'Em Slick

An interesting encounter, this battle allows you to use some slightly unconventional strategies. Your first objective is to destroy the Shattered Hand village west of your starting position. Use your Battleship to pulverize the Cannon Tower, then rush the village with your troops. Casualties may be high, but that's life (or death, in this case).

While the survivors sack the Shattered Hand encampment, put your Peasants to work building a base. Don't worry about a Shipyard until you have a Keep (or perhaps a Castle). Your first priority is expanding infrastructure. Immediately upgrade arrows and use Archers, backed by a couple of Guard Towers, to shoot down the occasional Dragon raider.

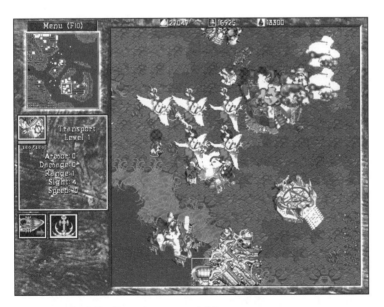

Figure 2.15 *Gryphons and Mages on a rampage*

Gold is abundant (two mines) on this peninsula, so build only the best units and max out the weapons upgrades. Gryphon Riders are the unit of choice. They fly anywhere, are invulnerable to most units, and have much better dental habits than Dragons.

While your peasants erect the Shipyard and accompanying maritime buildings, capture the Oil patch southeast of your base. Bypass the patch just south of your base—it's within range of Catapults and the Death Knights' Whirlwind.

As your Gryphon force grows, use it to secure a clear beach on the land mass just south of your base. Land at least two Transports full of ground forces there (including Mages). Once you've destroyed the Orc's Towers, send the Gryphons after enemy units.

Use the Mages' Blizzard on enemy concentrations and Polymorph on the truly dangerous animals. Nothing is more fun than Polymorphing a Dragon, or other vicious creature, into a harmless lamb.

☒ ☒ ☒ ☒ ☒ ☒

TIP *Peasants are an invaluable addition to your landing force. Use them to build Guard or Cannon Towers in the middle of the enemy village. Not only do the Towers give you a position on which to fall back, they destroy the village as well. Also, to shorten the training pipeline, it helps to build another, on-scene, Barracks.*

☒ ☒ ☒

By the time you capture and sack the Thunderlord village, your Gold Mines will be close to depleted. The island between you and the Laughing Skulls contains a good Mine. Send a boatload of Peasants to clear the forest on the isle's northeastern end and build

Figure 2.16 *Clearing the island for a Town Hall*

a Town Hall. Next, clear the wood from around the Mine and have yourself a golden time.

While you gather a force to assault the Laughing Skull village, flesh out your navy with several Battleships. Together with a force of Gryphons, these vessels can destroy the greenskin armada and their defending Towers. Once you eliminate these obstacles to invasion, use this combined air–sea force to soften up the enemy so you can land your troops with little difficulty. By this time, the Laughing Skulls have exhausted their gold supply and can't reinforce themselves. The battle now becomes a matter of leveling the village and mopping up.

Mission Nine

Heart of Evil

The towering spires of Shadowmoon reach upwards as obsidian blades to cleave the hostile amber skies above. The corrupt heart of the mighty Shaman's power is within reach. Press your attack and the bane of Ner'zuhl and his Order of Death Knights will be wiped from the face of Draenor forever.

By destroying this dark fortress and claiming the Book of Medivh, Khadgar will be able to close the rift and Azeroth will be rid of the Orcish Hordes forever!

Marching Orders

- ✖ **Objectives:** Destroy the Fortress of Shadowmoon. Raze the Mystic Runestones of Gul'dan.

- ✖ **Starting Location:** Central northern edge.

- ✖ **Enemy Location:** Shattered Hand clan—northwest; Thunderlord clan—southwest; Laughing Skull clan—southeast.

- ✖ **Resources:** Five Gold Mines—southwest, center, southeast and two northwest.

Daemons to Sheep

Initially, this is a tough battle. Your first objective is to move your forces east toward the Bonechewer village. Don't attack yet, however. Parade your forces past its northeastern Guard Tower and release the captives in the POW camp. *Now* you may attack. Use the Catapult to take out the Towers; use the Archers and footsoldiers to protect the Cat.

Once you've taken the village, destroy the enemy buildings and begin fabricating your own base. Surround the encampment with Guard Towers to defend against Dragons and raiding Death Knights. Train enough forces to garrison the camp and use the rest of your coin to build up base infrastructure. Upgrade all weapons and soldiers. Build a few Gnomish Flying Machines to scout the map, especially the central northern section, to locate your objectives. Make sure the Alliance army you train includes Gryphon Riders, Mages, several Ballistas, and the like. Leave some Archers and a few Gryphon Riders at home and take the rest of the entourage to ravage the Shattered Hand village.

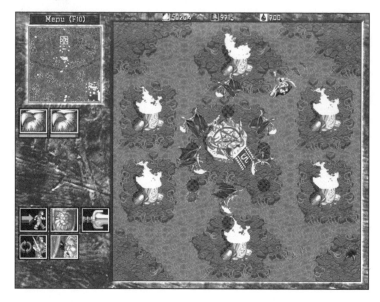

Figure 2.17 *The Mystic Runestones of Gul'dan and their keepers.*

Once again, lead with your Ballistas and take out the Towers guarding the village entrance. Use your Mages to either Polymorph the defenders or cast Blizzard in their midst. If you brought a sizable force, this township should fall without difficulty. Bring along Peasants to build a Barracks while your army sacks the village. For the next stage, you'll need several Rangers, so train them and task the Paladins with healing your wounded.

You can begin your advance on the village of the Bleeding Hollow and Shadowmoon clans by taking out the Undead guarding the entrance. Make a line of Rangers and Ballistas just south of the entrance Cannon Tower and crumble the structure with a hail of arrows.

Figure 2.18 *Rangers turn the Daemons into flying pincushions.*

Your Gnomish Flying Machines should already have found your main objective—the Mystic Sanctum of Ner'zhul. Six Daemons protect it.

Send in a Gryphon Rider to attack the Daemons and then retreat across your line of Rangers. While they let loose with deadly volleys of arrows, your Mages can Polymorph the Daemons into harmless beasts.

You may need to repeat this a couple of times to get all the bad guys. Once you've eliminated them, take out Ner'zhul and plunder the village. Stay alert—the Warsong Clan will counterattack from the east. Merely shield the units destroying the village and the glory of success will lie on your shoulders.

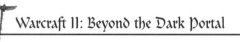

Mission Ten
The Battle of Hellfire

Although the Fortress of Ner'zuhl has been destroyed and the Death Knights scattered, neither the Shaman nor the Book of Medivh has been found. As Khadgar and Turalyon use their magiks to search the ruins for some clue as to the location of the mystic tome, a Gnomish flying machine descends, bringing news from the Hellfire peninsula and the Portal.

A multitude of Orcs have laid siege to the fortifications at Hellfire. Although the attacking warriors are not well equipped, their sheer numbers may spell the downfall of our forces there.

You must take command of the Alliance armies at Hellfire and break the siege before our troops are pushed back through the Dark Portal. We must withstand their charge long enough for the Book of Medivh to be recovered and the rift forever sealed.

Marching Orders

- ✠ **Objectives:** Outlast the besieging Orcs until lack of supplies forces them to retreat. All your Heroes must survive the siege.

- ✠ **Starting Location:** Southeast corner.

- ✠ **Enemy Location:** Shattered Hand clan—southwest; Thunderlord clan—north-center; Bonechewer clan—west-center.

🜨 **Resources:** Five Gold Mines—north-center, two west-center, one south-center and one southeast. One Oil patch northeast.

Creative Slaughter

This battle takes some creativity to win. Right from the beginning, you're under attack by three clans. The Shattered Hand clan primarily will send Ogres and Catapults with a few assorted Orcs or an occasional Death Knight. The Bonechewers will raid from the north with Grunts and Axethrowers. The Thunderlord clan, located north of your position, send only Dragons.

Your first priority is to expand your army. Quickly upgrade your Keep to a Castle and train Paladins, Gryphon Riders, Mages and Dwarven Demolition Squads. These will be your mainstay for victory. Use Gryphon Riders to attack Catapults and lower-grade units at a distance from the base. Position Mages near the outer walls so they can quickly Polymorph Ogres and Dragons that venture too near. Your Cannon and Guard Towers should take care of the rest with a minimal complement of lesser units. Use Paladins either to attack enemy units that break though or, more importantly, to heal the wounded. Gold is limited and the winner will be the commander who best conserves his resources—so break out them Band-Aids!

As your defenses stiffen and you can create extra units for offensive operations, target the Shattered Hand village. Gather six Demolition Squads, six Mages, four Paladins, and eight Gryphon Riders. Group each type of unit separately. Stop them beyond range of the village defenses. The Gryphons act as your air cover. The Paladins are the medics and last-resort support. Use the Dwarves to blow up the outer Towers.

Figure 2.19 *Dwarves rush in under cover of Gryphon Riders.*

Now send one Mage at a time to Polymorph an Ogre or other powerful enemy and quickly return to the Mage group. If enemy units follow, attack them with the Gryphons or other Mages. As the Mages clear the Orc units, send in more Dwarves to demolish the remaining Towers. Because they can attack your Gryphons, Guard Towers should be the priority. If units sustain damage, heal them between these short raids.

After destroying their defenses, move in to raze the village.

After you destroy the first village, you may need to bring up reinforcements, particularly Dwarven Demolition Squads. The Bonechewer town is next on the agenda. Use the same tactics and you should have no trouble. If there's still a Gold Mine, bring Peasants over, build a Town Hall, and mine away.

Your final objective is the Thunderlord village across the water. Their defenses are mainly Towers with a sprinkling of support units. They spent most of their resources on Dragons to raid your base. By this time, they're probably out of gold. To get across the water, you'll need to build a Shipyard, Foundry, and a Transport or two. Use your Gryphon Riders to secure a small beachhead, then send over a load of Demolition Squads. Use them to fell the Guard, Cannon Towers, and Catapults. The next load will be your Mages and Paladins. Polymorph the defenders and then level the village.

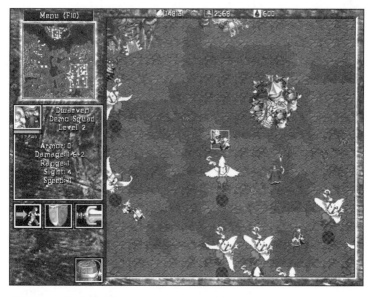

Figure 2.20 *The perfect team for storming an Orc village*

Mission Eleven

Dance of the Laughing Skull

You have proven your strength in battle, but none can stand against the combined might of the Horde. We of the Laughing Skull clan, however, seek advantage from the turmoil of this war. With the aid of your strongest warriors, our clan can gain dominance over the northern clans of Draenor.

Do not show surprise, Human—only the strongest survive within the Horde. You must secure the passes across the Blade's Edge Mountains and destroy the stronghold of the Thunderlord clan that dwell there. We will supply you with warriors and supplies culled from our villages. In return, we will give you the Book of Medivh, which we seized from Ner'zhul's stronghold before your armies could destroy it.

Marching Orders

- ☒ **Objective:** Destroy all enemy forces. All your Heroes must survive.

- ☒ **Starting Location:** Southeast corner, northeast corner.

- ☒ **Enemy Location:** Bonechewer clan—northwest corner; Thunderlord clan—south-center; Laughing Skull clan— northeast corner.

- ☒ **Resources:** Five Gold Mines—northwest corner, southwest corner, south-center, center, northeast corner.

Brother Against Brother

The challenge here is developing a strong defense while expanding your economic base. Your opponents, located west and south of you, usually conduct closely concurrent attacks. The fellows in the west favor Catapults, while the southerners will pitch in a couple of Death Knights for flavor. Coordinated attacks are a major headache in *Warcraft II*. You may be able to out-think the computer, but "out-mousing" it is a bit more dicey. Just when one front stabilizes, you realize all the units on the other front are dead.

The *good* news, though, is that a mountain range running roughly north–south down the entire map separates you from the greenskins. This range has only three gaps, and the enemy never

Figure 2.21 *A sturdy defense at the Western Gap*

seems to use the middle one. Furthermore, your opponent doesn't use Dragons—much to his dismay.

At the scenario's start, head north as fast as possible. Recruit the Orc village you enter and defeat a minor counterattack from the west. Build a wall of Farms across your side of the gap. These huts take a lot of damage and occasionally attract the attentions of opposing units. Behind these, erect two or three Cannon Towers to keep the attackers honest. Finally, form a reserve to attack Catapults when they trudge to the front.

Once you've stabilized this area, turn your attentions to the southern gap. After you defeat an attack by four Ogres, build two Guard Towers here and back them up with a few Knights. If you can get this stuff together you'll have no more worries from down south.

Once your defenses are ready, focus on the economics of expansion. Upgrade your troops and build a Fortress when possible. Your Gold Mine doesn't contain an infinite amount of gold, so send an expedition to plunder the Gold Mine south of the mountain's middle pass. Clear the area, build a Great Hall and Barracks. Both buildings will drastically reduce transit times for your units both to get to the front and to drop off resources.

Having stabilized the defense and economy, it's time to hit the offensive highway. The western Orc settlement should be the first to feel your wrath. Head out with two Ballistas, two Grunts, two Ogres, a pair of Death Knights, and Khadgar. Work the Death Knights, employing "Decay," and the Ballistas to break

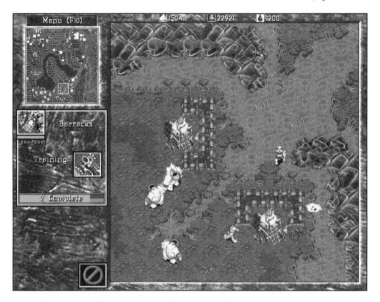

Figure 2.22 *Southern hospitality?*

down enemy defenses. Destroy the city, erect a Great Hall, and reap the spoils of victory.

This leaves the southern greenskins. Going directly south of the western village you'll find three Towers and a similar number of Ogres. Use your Ballista and Dragons to terminate this threat. Only the Tower in the center can touch the Dragons, so use the Ballista on this one. Watch out for Death Knights lurking in the shadows.

Once past the gates you won't encounter much organized resistance. However, exercise caution when mopping up this last village. A Death Knight might surprise you and assassinate one of your all-important Heroes. I hate it when that happens.

Mission Twelve

The Bitter Taste of Victory

Khadgar has discovered that although the Book of Medivh was stolen from Ner'zhul, the ancient Shaman has learned enough of its secrets to conjure his darkest spell. Over the blood red skies of Draenor, huge dimensional rifts appear, crackling with the cosmic energy of the Twisting Nether. Alleria's scouts report that Ner'zhul and his followers escaped through the largest of the new rifts as Draenor felt the first of its death throes. The tremendous energies emitted from the converging rifts have succeeded in breaking down the fabric of reality on Draenor; unleashing massive earth quakes and tidal waves upon its shores.

Unless the Dark Portal is closed on both worlds, Azeroth will be subject to an enormous backlash of energy resulting from Draenor's catastrophic discorporation.

Using the combined powers of the Book of Medivh and the Skull of Gul'dan, you must return Khadgar to the Dark Portal and seal the rift between Azeroth and the doomed world of Draenor, forever.

Marching Orders

- ❈ **Objectives:** Destroy the Dark Portal. (Only Khadgar can destroy the Dark Portal.) Khadgar must survive.

- ❈ **Starting Location:** North-center, southeast-center, and center (briefly).

- ✺ **Enemy Location:** Warsong clan—east-center; Bonechewer clan—center; Shadowmoon clan—northwest corner; Shattered Hand clan—south-center.

- ✺ **Resources:** Five Gold Mines—northwest, east-center, south-center, southeast corner, center.

The Final Frontier

March your northern forces to safety in the southeastern village. Have your Dwarves blow a hole in the mountains directly south of your position. Race through it to the village, ignoring all else.

As you run through the mountain pass, send your units south and a little east. When you get to the north–south mountain range, travel south down its east side. Once you reach the end, head southwest along another ridge until *it* ends. Make a U-turn and rush behind the comforting walls of your village. By the way, you'll pass three Peasants near this last mountain range; bring them along.

Take a breather as the Orcs destroy the rest of your center township. Start mining and cutting lumber. Build a Ballista and research upgrades at the Lumber Mill/Blacksmith's. Get your troops in order, because soon the unwashed masses will flood your village.

Make sure you have Footmen at the gate and the northern entrance to your encampment. Order them to Stand. As the first Orcs arrive, have Khadgar unleash a Blizzard on their approach path. This is great stuff—10 to 15 Orcs will die without ever touching you. As the Blizzard fades, send your Gryphon to kill the Catapult moving up to pound your tightly packed units. This should blunt the Orc offensive.

Now develop your Portal assault and building strategy. The Portal is in the town west of your position. Have Khadgar destroy it

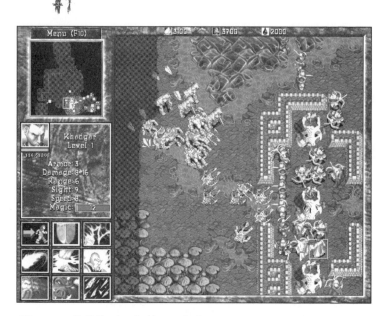

Figure 2.23 *A chilling defense*

and you've won. Because of this, there's no need for a 30-year plan. Focus on immediate unit improvements and building Guard Towers to counter periodic Dragon attacks.

The assault party should advance in an organized fashion (as organized as you can get these guys). Move forward until you can anchor your Footmen between the forest and the Orc's Blacksmith. Have your Knights set up across the north side of this salient connecting the Blacksmith to the mountains. Your Archers should fill in behind the Footmen and Knights. Bring the Magicians and Ballista through the center. Command all units to Stand.

Once this position is set, roll the Ballista around to attack the first Tower south of the Portal. Extend your defensive line to cover the Ballista. Cast Blizzard on the Peons attempting to rebuild the

Tower you're destroying. Use these techniques to level the other Towers in the village and fight off the constant Orc counterattacks.

By now, there won't be much armed resistance left, just a huge gaggle of Peons.

Set up a defensive perimeter and order Khadgar to destroy the Portal. Unfortunately, this takes darn-near forever. Bring a couple of Peasants over to build a Town Hall, Barracks, and several Towers to assist in your perimeter defense.

That's it. Now it's just a waiting game. Eventually the Portal falls and you can sleep soundly, knowing you saved the world.

Figure 2.24 *The Alliance arrayed in front of the Orcs' village*

Chapter Three

The Orcish Hordes

Mission One

Slayer of the Shadowmoon

Though the Elder Shaman Ner'zhul holds the rank of Warchief of Draenor, your position as Slayer to the Shadowmoon clan places the duty of leading their armies into battle upon your head.

Ner'zhul has discovered how the rift was first formed and now covets the idea of not only reopening the gateway into Azeroth, but of creating new portals and seeking out even more worlds to control.

You must subjugate an order of Death Knights who have secured the knowledge needed to rebuild the Dark Portal. The renegade Ogre-Mage Mogor, of the Laughing Skull clan, has taken control of these dark soldiers and is seeking to create a powerful spell with the aid of their necromantic magic. His life is also forfeit.

Although we have no Dragons to command, we have learned that Grom Hellscream, leader of the Warsong clan, has been captured by the Laughing Skull and is being held prisoner. Free him and he will surely aid in your battles.

Marching Orders

- ✠ **Objectives:** Destroy the Death Knights and their Temple. Grom Hellscream must survive.

- ✠ **Starting Location:** Southeast corner.

- ✠ **Enemy Location:** Various. Temple of the Damned and Ogre-Mage Mogor are located in the northern center of the map.

- ✠ **Resources:** There are no Gold Mines in this scenario.

To Kill an Ogre

Although the scenario provides no Mines, what you initially see is not what you get. As you travel, you'll find new forces to strengthen your horde. Nevertheless, conserving strength is important. The starting forces are tough enough to deal with most encounters, but the casualties taken in doing so directly affect the outcome of the battle for the Temple.

Keeping this in mind, it's time to set out on our quest. Place the Death Knight in the rear of your party to prevent his untimely demise at the hands of Undead ambushers. Proceed to the mid-southwest area of the map and free the Trolls residing there.

Leaving the Axethrower's small village, head northwest, killing the Undead as you go. Soon you will bump into Grom Hellscream, eager to join up and ready to "slice and dice." Continue toward the

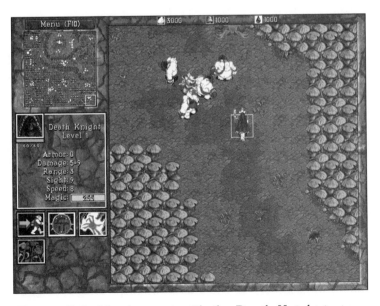

Figure 3.1 *Heading out with the Death Knight in tow*

top of the map until you stumble on a small village containing a Lumber Mill. Use the Lumber Mill to upgrade the troll's axes . . . you'll need a sharp blade soon: Another stash of Trolls and some Goblin Sappers wait just north of the Lumber Mill.

Before you press on to the Temple, heal the Death Knight. Remember, when Death Coil is cast on living entities, the Knight gets stronger. These beings don't have to be the enemy, although they can't be friendlies. This leaves the Red Beasts. For each of these the Knight zaps, he'll receive three health points, so take time to kill any you find grazing the pastures of Draenor.

It's possible to tackle the end game, and gain access to the Death Knight's Temple, in either of two ways: 1) Use the Sappers to blast through the rock formation to the east of the Lumber Mill. 2) Bypass the rock formation and attack the Temple from the east. Certainly the blow-and-go option is the most direct. If most of your

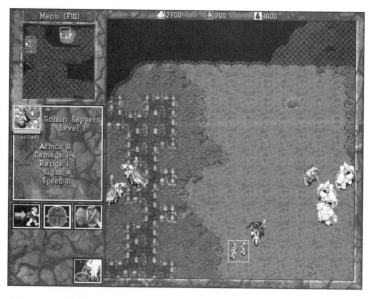

Figure 3.2 The sappers prepare to breach the wall.

initial force remains alive, this is the preferred method. If your Horde looks a little sickly, continue south of the formation. You'll get into the scenario's biggest fracas here, but it's winnable. Keep the Sappers and Death Knight to the rear and wade in with Grunts, Ogres, and Axethrowers. Use the Death Knight's Death Coil to assist the frontline troopers—particularly Grom Hellscream. Once you defeat the enemy Orcs and Trolls, free the friendlies in the corral to the right of the rocks.

Now it's high noon at the O.K. Corral. Advance west toward the Death Knight Temple. Use the Sappers to breach the wall. Zap Mogor's Knights with your own, and when they sally forth to give battle, kill them with your Ogres, Trolls, and Hellscream. Grom is one hell of a fighter, but he *can* be killed, so keep an eye on him. If his health bar falls into the mid-yellow range, pull him back.

After you slay the Death Knights, tiptoe into the compound, Knight to the rear, remaining Ogres in front. Ogre-Mage Mogor will come forth ready to rumble. Occupy him with your Ogres (or whatever infantry is left) and use the Death Knight for the kill. Now it's merely a matter of destroying the Temple and victory is yours—point, set, and match.

METZEN · 95

Mission Two

The Skull of Gul'dan

The skull of Gul'dan is a powerful artifact and essential for resurrecting the Dark Portal. A pathetic Orc Captain of the Bonechewer clan wears the skull as a symbol of his station and does not know of its true power.

Ner'zhul has sent the Ogre hero, Dentarg, to influence warriors from the Thunderlord clan to join in the battle against the Bonechewers. You will also be assisted by the warriors of the Shattered Hand and their leader Korgath Bladefist.

Move quickly to the Thunderlord village and raise an army to crush the Bonechewer Captain and win the Skull of Gul'dan.

Marching Orders

- **Objective:** Capture the villiage controlled by the Thunderlord clan. Destroy the Bonechewer Captain and his encampment.

- **Starting Location:** Northwest corner of the map.

- **Enemy Location:** Mideastern edge.

- **Resources:** Gold: Four Mines—northwest, southwest, northeast, mideast.

Victory to the Bold

This one is a tad tougher than "Slayer of the Shadowmoon." The Orc starts with Dentarg and one Grunt. He must build his forces rapidly and raze the enemy settlement.

The key is aggression. A passive player will go bankrupt attempting to slow down the persistent Bonechewer raids. However, season the aggression with a dash of prudence. Headlong assaults won't work. Instead, you must defeat the enemy little by little.

Here's one way:

Split up Dentarg and the Grunt. Send the Ogre to the southwest corner of the map to recruit the Thunderlords living there. Meanwhile, walk the Grunt southeast to enlist Korgath Bladefist (located at the Blacksmith east of the Mine at the western map edge), and subsequently his Axethrowers.

Divvy up your newfound allies to guard the north and east entrances of the southern village. Immediately train 10 to 12 Peons. Eight should mine while the remainder work on the woods in the northeast corner of the settlement. Keep an eye on these guys—cutting completely through the woods will open an avenue of attack for the bad guys.

Build two Barracks. Place one next to each village entrance to cut down the time reinforcements take to reach the "gates." When gold allows, start churning out troops. Build a Lumber Mill and upgrade the watchtowers to Guard or Cannon towers. As soon as it's practical, erect a Stronghold and Ogre Mound.

By now—usually before the Stronghold or Ogre Mound are fashioned—the bad guys have come calling . . . and calling, and calling. Don't panic. Your Cannon Towers, aided by three Grunts and a couple of Axethrowers, usually can buy time to assemble a counterattack force. Once a small force of Grunts, Ogres (if you

Figure 3.3 *The initial north gate defense*

have them), Peons, and Axethrowers, supported by a catapult, has been assembled, exit the east village entrance and attack northeast.

The Bonechewers react strongly. The path runs thick with green blood. Hopefully, you'll make it to the lower reaches of their settlement and lay waste to a couple of Farms. Don't push it! Plenty of Ogres and Guard Towers remain, waiting to liquidate your troops.

When the attack loses momentum, call it off. Use the Peons to build a new Barracks near your spearhead and start training replacements for the depleted attack force.

Meanwhile, gold may be running short. Before it gets critical, send a Peon task force, escorted by Grunts, to the Mine at the western map edge. Build a Great Hall and commence gathering loot. If you keep the pressure up on the southern front, the bad guys will probably leave this little mining expedition alone.

Now winning is just a matter of chipping away at the Bonechewer village. Build plenty of Catapults and Ogres. The Catapults are great for taking out Guard and Cannon Towers, enjoying a slight range advantage over both. Ogres are great for taking out anything else. Continue to use the attack–regroup strategy. Capture the southern enemy Gold Mine as soon as you find it, limiting the computer's ability to replace its forces. Once the large east-north-eastern settlement has been raised, send your Hordes to the southeast corner to eliminate the last vestiges of the enemy clan.

A final note: Although it may be possible, given the length of time it takes to win, to upgrade the Stronghold to Fortress and construct a Temple of the Damned or Altar of Storms, it isn't necessary. You may, however, want to give it a try as an alternative.

Figure 3.4 Initial bad guys defense

Mission Three

Thunderlord and Bonechewer

Ner'zhul has met with opposition to his plans from the leaders of both the Thunderlord and Bonechewer clans. They desire to journey to Azeroth and have their clans triumph where Doomhammer had failed. This is a vision not shared by your Warchief...

You are to lead the forces of Shadowmoon against the strongholds of both Bonechewer and Thunderlord. Once these weak fools and their clans are removed, no others will dare to interfere with the dark schemes of Ner'zuhl.

Marching Orders

- ✖ **Objectives:** Destroy the Thunderlord clan.
  Destroy the Bonechewer clan.

- ✖ **Starting Location:** Just east of center map (in a northish kind of way).

- ✖ **Enemy Location:** Everywhere (specifically northwest, southwest, northeast, and southeast). Bonechewer clan—south, Thunderlord clan—north.

- ✖ **Resources:** Five Gold Mines—northwest, southwest, northeast, southeast, and just east of center map (in a northish kind of way). You ought to see this one right off—it's in your camp.

Lookin' for Green Blood

Obviously any scenario, in any game, will have its key elements. "Thunderlord and Bonechewer" is no different. You must remember three things to make green ham sandwiches out of the Thunderlords—build Cannon Towers, build Catapults, and train Ogres. The Ogres and Catapults will be the mainstays of any assault force you send out. The Cannon Towers will be the mainstay of your survival.

You start surrounded by your rival Orcish brethren. These guys are all lookin' for your blood. You'll best discourage them by rapidly constructing a Lumber Mill and upgrading the Scout Towers to Guard status. As the cash flow increases, build another Guard Tower to protect the encampment's northern entrance. This should hold back the Smorgishborgs for a while.

Figure 3.5 *The initial base camp defense*

With the base saved from destruction and currency in the coffers, it's time to build a Blacksmith and grow a Cannon Tower next to the Great Hall. The cannon, with its longer range, serves as a suitable backup to the previously placed Guard Towers.

Next, upgrade the Hall, pile up a mound of Ogres, and use any pocket change for weapon improvements. This lays the foundation for the next phase.

Handle the constant Bonechewer raids with the least possible force, preferably Grunts and Axethrowers. Despite this constant pressure, train a counterattack force of five to seven Ogres, two Catapults, and a pair of Axethrowers.

Send these guys northeast toward the Mine located in that map quadrant. Lead with the Cats and screen them with foot soldiers.

Figure 3.6 *The push north: Cats in the lead, protected by Ogres.*

Secure the Mine and set up shop. This camp should include a Barracks, Great Hall, and two Cannon Towers. Once the Towers are operational, send the Cats home. You'll need them to raze the southeastern Orc village.

Of course, while you've been off leveling the neighborhood, things haven't been quiet at home. The raids continue (can't these guys take a hint?). However, if you have enough structures heaving spears and spitting cannon balls at the intruders, they usually get the worst of it.

Take time to groom another strike force. Send these green-skins southeast, kill the Orcs, flatten their buildings, and steal the gold. In addition to the normal camp accouterments (Great Hall, Barracks, and the like) you'll need a Goblin Alchemist for the coming end game.

Here's how that tune plays. Train a Horde at the initial village and one in the southeast. Recruit three Gobblin Sapper squads and move them, with the southeastern troops, to the east edge of the north—south woods separating the camp from the Bonechewer city. Blow a path through the forest. As the last trees are cleared, roll south with the base-camp Horde. They'll hit the Bonechewers about the same time as the eastern gaggle pours out of the woods. This should be enough to chill the heart of even the toughest motherboard.

After the majority of the Bonechewers' Towers fall silent, let the Peons build a couple of Cannon Towers to demolish the rest of the city while you commence refitting the army.

The final portion of this encounter is simple. Take your time, by now the Thunderlords' last Mine has collapsed and they aren't getting any stronger. Lead a force thick with Cats and Ogres north, chipping away at Thunderlord defenses. Again, construct Cannon Towers to handle mop-up.

Mission Four

The Rift Awakened

From the ranks of the Death Knights comes Teron Gorefiend. The death of Gul'dan places these dark horsemen under the authority of no clan, but Gorefiend shares Ner'zhul's desire to open numerous portals. He offers his influence over the Death Knights of Draenor in exchange for a world the Death Knights can claim as their own.

Using both the knowledge gained at the defeat of the Ogre-Mage Mogor and the necromantic powers of the Death Knights, Ner'zhul successfully awakens the arcane energies of the mystic rift. As you lead the forces of Shadowmoon into Azeroth, a Human battlement, constructed to keep the portal closed, stands before you. Destroy this Citadel and claim the lands surrounding the rift.

Marching Orders

- **✖ Objectives:** Destroy the Humans. Teron must survive.

- **✖ Starting Location:** North-center.

- **✖ Enemy Location:** Northwest, southwest, and center.

- **✖ Resources:** Five Gold Mines—northwest, midwestern map-edge, southwest, center, and southeast.

Goldilocks and the Three Nations of Man

I'll say it right up front—this guide takes some of the fun out of this scenario. As the Orc Leader, you're faced with destroying three Human settlements. One, the nation of Azeroth, is way too powerful to engage at the beginning of the scenario. A second, the nation of Dalaran, is way too far away. The third, like Baby Bear's bed in the tale of Goldilocks, is just right. These unfortunate men belong to the nation of Kul Tiras and are ripe for the plucking.

A lot of the fun in "The Rift Awakened" is in locating the weak Humans, attacking them, and moving on. However, with this book, you already know where to go. Doesn't seem fair does it? But, as I've said, war is tremendously inconsiderate.

The opening moves are easy: Get the Goblin Zeppelin away from the Elvin Archers and attack those same Archers (and their attendant city) with everything else. Make five groups- from the initial war party: Catapults, Axethrowers, Ogres, Grunts and Teron Gorefiend, and Peons. Don't forget to lead with your Catapults. This may sound odd, but they have the greatest weapon and sight range (excluding the Zeppelin).

☒ ☒ ☒ ☒ ☒ ☒

TIP *Catapults hold a slight range advantage over both Guard and Cannon towers. Direct the Catapults to attack these towers while still out of range and the wooden behemoths will stop and fire at max range—outdistancing the towers. Use the foot soldiers to protect the Catapults from Alliance infantry and cavalry.*

☒ ☒ ☒

After securing the Kul Tiras village, build five Pig Farms and a Great Hall. Place the Pig Farms to partially block the passage between patches of woods to the south-southeast. A lot of action takes place there and the less area you must defend, the better. Once you build the farms, buy into a Lumber Mill—put it next to the southeast woods—and a Blacksmith. Now you're set to build three Cannon Towers (two guarding the southeast approach, one sighted directly down the throat of the southern approach).

After basic village-tending, upgrade the weapons and Great Hall. Build an Ogre Mound, Ogres, and, if you have the money, a Temple of the Damned. Don't sit around and wait for the money to accumulate, however. As soon as you can amass an 8- to 12-unit task force of Ogres, Axethrowers, and Catapults, move south.

Figure 3.7 An assault on the Northwest Village— the Catapults lead the way

METZEN · 55

Figure 3.8 *Storming the midwestern mine*

Capture the Mine midway down, build another Great Hall, and start some serious gold reaping.

Next stop is the Dalaranian village due south. You'll find plenty of Guard and Cannon towers from here on in, so you may want to have at least five Catapults in the assault force. A good mix is five Catapults, five Ogres, four Axethrowers, and three Death Knights. Take some time to research "Decay." It's awesome against men and materiel alike. Don't waste time upgrading the Ogres to Mages.

Build a Great Hall and Barracks near the ex-Dalaranian Mine and refit your forces. The next phase is a tough one. The forces of Azeroth are numerous and firm believers in Cannon Towers. Again, you must use Catapults and Death Knights to soften up the defenses before the Ogres wade in for the final assault. Concentrate first on knocking out Churches, Town Halls, and Barracks; this will cripple the Humans' ability to regenerate.

☒ ☒ ☒ ☒ ☒ ☒

TIP *Because the scenario's objective is to destroy the wretched Humans completely, you could spend a lot of time mopping up. This is a great time to steal a page from the original Warcraft II strategy guide. Construct a couple of Cannon Towers in the middle of the remnants of a Human village and they'll open up on everything in sight, effectively leveling the city.*

☒ ☒ ☒

Once you've crushed the final Stronghold of Azeroth, there's nothing left but to find and slay the few remaining Humans. Don't get too cocky. Cockiness wastes time. Ensure that the hunting parties have sufficient force to handle whatever they find. A mix of five or six units usually does the trick.

Mission Five

Dragons of Blackrock Spire

When the Horde was driven back into the Black Morass, it was able to take only a small portion of its forces through the Dark Portal before the Portal was destroyed. Because the Alliance had rescued the Dragon Queen Alexstrasza and captured the Dragonmaw clan, you were no longer able to command these great winged beasts.

As you secure the rift and begin constructing a new portal, a haggard Grunt approaches your encampment. His uniform marks him as a warrior of the Bleeding Hollow clan. He tells how those of his clan who failed to return through the Portal eluded capture and imprisonment by the Alliance armies. You also learn that many once-enslaved Dragons continue to feed upon the Humans and now roost at Blackrock Spire. If you can break through the Human defenses and gain the trust of these creatures, perhaps you can bring Ner'zhul powerful allies.

Marching Orders

- **Objectives:** Capture as many Dragons as possible. Capture the Dragons' Roost high in the mountains.

- **Starting Location:** Southwest corner of the map.

- **Enemy Location:** Mid-southwest, northwest, and middle-ish. Roost is at northeastern corner.

- **Resources:** Six Gold Mines—southwest (two), northwest, north-center, mideast, southeast.

Beans and Bullets

You gotta eat, and you gotta pay the troops. These facts are a couple of keys to this scenario. Although the Orc starts off with a powerful Horde, he doesn't own the Farms to feed them. Consequently, any further training must be put on hold until you build Farms sufficient to feed the greenskins. The Humans, on the other hand, need the Gold Mine just north of your location to finance a strong army.

First, build Farms. Detail a Peon to start right away while the other two mine. Raise the initial Farm at the southeastern edge of the village (below the woods) to block potential invaders.

After beating back the Human probe on the town's east side, take two Ogres, seven Grunts, and three Axethrowers through the

Figure 3.9 *Taking the Human's gold—the orcs raid the mine just above their base camp.*

Figure 3.10 *Born free! The freed Dragons turn on the Elves at the scenario's end.*

same passage. Turn north at the first opportunity and continue until you reach the southeast corner of the Human settlement just north of your camp. Capture the Mine located there; however, don't move west of the Mine—it will draw a strong Human response.

This attack is crucial to ultimate victory. Possessing the Mine doubles your gold flow and reduces the Humans' income. Plus, your losses bring your forces' nutritional needs more in line with their farming capacity.

You may expand the work force (at the original camp) to 10 Peons, now, and set up a Lumber Mill, build four Towers, and upgrade them to Guard status (so the Griffin Riders will think twice about getting too close).

As soon as resources permit, raise a Great Hall near the northern Mine. This should shore up orc finances. As the money pours in, build a Blacksmith, two Barracks, upgrade the southern Great Hall twice (to Fortress), an Ogre Mound, and Temple of the Damned. Research Decay and train a strike force of three Catapults, six Ogres, three Axethrowers, and three Death Knights.

March north, sweeping all before you. Obviously, this group will need constant reinforcement. However, using the general tips given in the front of the book, this Horde should smash the Humans' two western settlements—destroying the pesky Griffin Aviaries as it goes.

☒ ☒ ☒ ☒ ☒ ☒

NOTE *A word on this northern excursion. It's not absolutely necessary to crush the northernmost Human settlement to save the Dragons. However, if you choose to go for the (somewhat) middle-of-the-map Gold Mine first, you'll constantly be forced to fend off attacks on your rear. It's best to get the Humans out of the way first, and then attend to business.*

☒ ☒ ☒

After leveling the northernmost settlement, proceed east to the Mine located in the northern middle of the map. If necessary, you may stop here to regroup, build a Great Hall, Barracks, and, if needed, a Temple of the Damned. Slaughter the remaining Human enclave east of the Mine, head to the Dragon Roost (northeastern map edge), and carry the day.

Mission Six
New Stormwind

Finding the survivors of the Bleeding Hollow clan and gaining the Dragon Deathwing as an ally has strengthened your position in Azeroth. Your success has not gone unnoticed by Ner'zhul. He rewards your victories by assigning you a dangerous mission.

Gorefiend has sensed a focus of arcane energies within a castle that has been raised upon the foundations of Stormwind Keep. Ner'zhul believes that this can only be the fabled Book of Medivh. Only a fool would leave such power unguarded, so your assault upon the new Stormwind castle will be a bloody one . . .

Marching Orders

- **Objectives:** Destroy everything.
  Terron must survive.
- **Starting Location:** Southeast corner of the map.
- **Enemy Location:** Villages are in the southwest and northwest corners. Outposts are located in various other locations.
- **Resources:** Four Gold Mines—southeast,southwest, northwest, and mideast (east of pond).

Love Them Lizards

Winning strategy for Mission Six can be summed up in four words—Dragons, Gold, and Guard Towers. This encounter is primarily an air war. There may be other ways to win it, but using Dragons is the easiest. As with any scenario, especially those with high-cost units, keeping the gold river running is critical. Without a lot of capital, it's darn-near impossible to build and maintain a credible air force. Finally, until those Dragons are airborne, the primary defense against the not-so-pathetic Gryphon Riders is Guard Towers.

Keeping this in the forefront of our green skulls, let's get down to killing some Human scum. Click first on the Great Hall; upgrade

Figure 3.11 Axethrowers employed as a mobile anti-Gryphon battery.

it. Remember, you want Dragons, and lots of them, this scenario. The sooner you can build Dragon Roosts the better. The Stronghold upgrade is Step One.

☒ ☒ ☒ ☒ ☒ ☒

NOTE *While we're on the subject of clicking, try poking Terron about 10 times in a row. It's good for a chuckle.*

☒ ☒ ☒

Step Two: Send the three Peons to mine southwest of the Great Hall. Group nine Axethrowers and send them to the pass northwest of the Great Hall. Place the remaining Grunts and Ogres in front of them. Issue the "Stand Ground" order to them all. Pair Terron with an Axethrower and place them slightly behind the other troopers.

Use the Axethrowers as a mobile anti-Gryphon battery. You'll need the Grunts and Ogres to block an assault through the northwest corridor, and Terron is the reserve.

☒ ☒ ☒ ☒ ☒ ☒

NOTE *Use Terron's Death Coil to terminate Gryphon Riders previously weakened by the Axethrowers. This will buff up the Death Knight's health.*

☒ ☒ ☒

Build and train four Guard Towers and seven (for a total of 10) Peons during the game's initial phase. Use three of the emerald-

Figure 3.12 *Desert Storm revisited! Dragons soften up the southwestern stronghold.*

colored laborers to chop wood; the rest can mine. The Guard Towers should keep the Gryphons at bay. Because axes are such key weapons early on, upgrade them as soon as possible.

Village defenses are stable and cashflow is steady. Now gather a strike force to capture the northeastern Mine—five Axethrowers, an Ogre, Terron, and a Grunt or two should do the job. Trail them with two Peons and march north. As soon as you secure the Mine build a Great Hall and Barracks.

Now comes the midgame—perhaps the most crucial period of the scenario. In the northern camp build four Guard Towers (again, for Gryphon-shooting) and a second Great Hall, train Peons, and make money—*lots* of money. In the southern camp, make an Ogre Mound and, again, lots of money. Once you establish a solid line of capital it's time to upgrade the southern Stronghold to Fortress, erect an Alchemist building, and start building Dragon Roosts in the north.

These Roosts are *the key* to the scenario. From this point on, devote 90 percent of your effort to pumping out Dragons. Start with three Roosts in the north. As your income permits, build more. By scenario end you should have seven or eight (and the income to keep them spewing winged lizards). As you train Dragons send them down to the southern camp. Don't use them to fight off the incessant Gryphon attacks; that's what Axethrowers and Guard Towers are for. You must build up a squadron of Dragons in the lower camp. While the flapping fire-breathers accumulate, train three Goblin Sappers, a couple of Ogres, Axethrowers, and Grunts.

Now, it's roasting time.

Fly your squadron of Dragons west to the Human Stronghold. Use them to level the defenses. Follow with Sappers, Ogres, and so on, trailed by two Peons. Have the Sappers blow through the rock surrounding the village and use the other infantry to mop up any resistance. Bring in the Peons, construct a Great Hall, and commence accumulating gold.

The rest is relatively easy. By now you should have seven or eight Roosts and the capital (three Mines) to keep them employed. Do nothing but make Dragons. Fly to the northeast corner and smash the men of Azeroth residing there. Then send your winged minions to fry any stragglers.

Mission Seven

The Seas of Azeroth

After taking the castle of New Stormwind, you search in vain for the Book of Medivh. As you sift through the rubble of the fallen city, you find the corpse of a Footman with a Human dagger in his side.

The spies of the Bleeding Hollow clan confirmed that this blade was crafted by the weapon smiths of Alterac. These Humans are the same that were willing to betray their own brothers, and it may be that they have stolen the Book of Medivh for their own purposes.

They will regret their decision . . .

To journey to Alterac, you must first establish naval superiority over the warships of the Alliance. The base at Kul Tiras has always been the Human's key to the might of their armada. You must establish a strong presence in the Great Sea in order to destroy Kul Tiras and prepare you way into the Alterac.

Marching Orders

- **Objectives:** Build five Shipyards. Destroy all enemy ships.

- **Starting Location:** Mideastern near edge.

- **Enemy Location:** Nation of Azeroth, southeast; Nation of Kul Tiras, center island—both northeastern islands.

- **Resources:** Four Gold Mines—northeastern island, center island, eastern and southern mainland. Five Oil splotches—north-center, center (two), southwest-center, southwest.

Death from Above

Yo, who says you need a powerful navy to control the ocean? The Germans nearly pulled it off in World War II with nothing but some U-boats and bombers. Imagine what they could have done with Dragons! This scenario is winnable with no more than a five- or six-ship navy. Just follow along, matey—or should I say flyboy?

Once again, your first priorities are Lumber Mills and Guard and Cannon towers. The pathetic Humans have a couple of Aviaries on the northwestern island and, in tune with their consistently inconsiderate nature, will constantly pound your defenses with Gryphon Riders—at least until you get enough spear-chucking anti-Gryphon systems online.

Figure 3.13 Part of the L-shaped line of death

Figure 3.14 *Searching for those pesky Submarines*

Send a squad of Grunts north to eliminate the warriors there. Then construct an L-shaped string of alternating Cannon and Guard towers starting at the northern inlet and hooking under your village. This stabilizes the situation and gives you some much-needed time to concentrate on the economic betterment of your forces.

Focus your energies on two items—cash and Dragons. Dragons are beautiful reptiles—fierce, fast, and they don't molt nearly as bad as Gryphons. Nevertheless, they take a ton of cash to subjugate (must be all the trainers they ingest), so you'll need big-time cash flow to support your winged habit. Sink the dough into about five Dragon Roosts. With a herd of Dragons on hand, establish local bestial flying superiority over your encampment and the surrounding waters.

Now erect two Shipyards, an Oil Refinery, and a Foundry. Drill for oil at the northern splotch. Yeah, the one to the east is a lot closer but, without any jousting tournaments to keep them occupied, the Humans on the center island will make you pay dearly for using it.

Make a small task force—a Juggernaught (I love that word—"Barkeep, give me another Juggernaught"), two Destroyers, and matched Transports loaded with Ogres and Peons. Send these ships, escorted by six to nine Dragons, to the northwestern island. Use the Dragons, Juggernaughts, and Destroyers to level the defenses. Land the Ogre Marines to mop up, the Peons to raise a Great Hall, and a couple of Cannon Towers to open up on surviving Human structures.

You must spend this additional income on three shipyards (remember, you need a total of five) and more Dragons. Group a bunch of air lizards (nine is ideal) and make a courtesy call on all the paleskins' flotillas, sending them to the bottom. That's it. Well, almost. The ape-like creatures have a couple of Submarines sneaking about. Split the Dragon squadron and have them patrol the ocean in a crisscross pattern.

Soon they'll flush the Subs and the scenario will end.

Navy? Hey, we don't need no stinkin' navy.

Mission Eight

Assault on Kul Tiras

Now that you have cleared a path to the island of Kul Tiras, you must send your wave riders against the core of the Human fleet. With the naval forces of the Humans defeated, the Horde will have free reign of the Great Sea. We have also learned that Admiral Proudmoore is no longer a member of the Alliance and does not have the support of their armies. Remove his armada and Kul Tiras will fall.

Marching Orders

- ☣ **Objectives**: Destroy the armada of Kul Tiras. Destroy Kul Tiras.

- ☣ **Starting Location:** Crammed together on the barren eastern isle.

- ☣ **Enemy Location:** Kul Tiras Village is north-center, naval base is center, and the accursed Aviaries are in the northwest corner.

- ☣ **Resources:** Six Gold Mines—southwestern island, mainland north-center (two), map center (three—one southwest of center, one north of center, and one center). Two Oil splotches in ocean canal.

Invading the Mainland

The first thing you must do is get everyone the heck out of Dodge—eastern Dodge, that is. The eastern island is nowheresville. Load up the Transports and go west, young Orc. Use a two-Destroyer, two-Juggernaught, single-Dragon screen, placed north of the eastern island, to keep the Humies away from your convoy.

When you arrive at your new home, build a Great Hall and five or six Farms. Keep the Axethrowers grouped together in their "mobile anti-Gryphon battery" formation. As soon as possible build a few Guard Towers to keep the overly eager Gryphon Riders at bay.

With the home fires well tended, load the Transports with three Peons, half the remaining Trolls, and the Death Knight. Sail across

Figure 3.15 *The Orcish naval buildup*

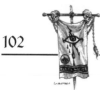

the inlet, land these Marines, and head for the south-center Mine. Build a big-time base here. Include an Ogre Mound (possible from an upgrade of the Great Hall at the original base), three Dragon Roosts, a couple of Barracks, and a Temple of the Damned. Use the serious coin you should be pulling to upgrade all weapons and start a naval base at your southern paradise. An Oil Refinery, Foundry, and two Shipyards will do the trick. Build a medium task force—about two Juggernaughts with a six-Destroyer escort.

It's important not to go into nautical construction overdrive because any ships left after you've scuttled the Kul Tiras navy will be wasted. Send this flotilla, along with a half-dozen Dragons, against the Kul Tiras naval base.

Regroup, refit, give the Grunts a weekend pass. Concentrate on gathering a well-rounded force. Make sure, though, that you have plenty of Death Knights, Cats, and Dragons.

Send the flying reptiles on a surgical strike to the Aviaries in the northwest corner, seriously flattening Kul Tiras air power for the foreseeable future.

With the air power knocked back, begin a slow but steady encroachment on Human territory. Go for the two center Mines next. Use your ranged weapons extensively.

❦ ❦ ❦ ❦ ❦ ❦

NOTE *The adventurous may choose to go for the western Humans first. Use Goblin Sappers to blow a hole through the east–west woods and fall on the enemy's flank. This has the advantage of attacking the Kul Tirasians' soft underbelly, but it's harder to reinforce.*

❦ ❦ ❦

Figure 3.16 *The attack force mustered at the Ex-Kul Tiras Naval Base*

✠ ✠ ✠ ✠ ✠ ✠

TIP *Death Knights can be especially tough when working together. One casts Unholy Armor on his compatriot. While so protected the second Death Knight moves within Death and Decay range of a significant structure and casts the spell—immune from return fire.*

✠ ✠ ✠

At first the going is exceedingly tough. Just keep refitting and moving forward. Each Mine you capture lessens the Humans' ability to match your builds.

☒ ☒ ☒ ☒ ☒ ☒

TIP *Beserkers with regenerative ability do well in this type of battle. Once they take a few hits, roll them to the rear where they can recover their health.*

☒ ☒ ☒

Eventually you'll win the war of attrition, wiping out the Humans' center. Then it's merely a matter of turning west and taking out the remaining structures.

☒ ☒ ☒ ☒ ☒ ☒

CAUTION *Although a reckless advance loses the Orcs more men and materiel than they can afford to replace, moving too slowly is just as lethal. A large Horde needs a lot of money. If you fail to add new Gold Mines to your inventory, bankruptcy will beat you long before the Humans do.*

☒ ☒ ☒

Mission Nine

The Tomb of Sargeras

Now that the Great Sea is once again under the dominion of our wave riders, Ner'zhul has come upon a plan to increase the powers of the Dark Portal. While he was the tutor of Gul'dan, the Shaman bound their souls so that he could keep watch over his disciple. Even though Gul'dan knew that this link would serve to inform Ner'zhul of the Warlock's studies with the spirits that dwelt in the Twisting Nether, he was too arrogant to care.

Ner'zhul has ordered you to lead a small band to the tomb in order to find the Jeweled Scepter of Sargeras. The remains of the Stormreaver and Twilight's Hammer encampment surround the entrance to the tomb and the howling of their tortured souls fill the air. Although the inhabitants of this place died long ago, their bodies have been torn from earthen graves by the vile magiks of the Daemons and made to stalk this region for all eternity.

Marching Orders

- ⚔ **Objective:** Slay the Daemon who guards the Jeweled Scepter of Sargeras.

- ⚔ **Starting Location:** Southwest corner.

- ⚔ **Enemy Location:** You name it, they're everywhere. However, the Daemon is at west-center of the map.

- ⚔ **Resources:** Shipyard at the port; Temple of the Damned on Mage Isle; Lumber Mill on the eastern land mass; Blacksmith found along the trail.

The Slaying of a Daemon

These no-Gold-Mine scenarios are unique in the Warcraft genre. Normally, everything you do is rushed—not so here. Take all day, no one cares except your spouse. You're still going to meet the same people and fight the same battles.

Before starting out, place the Grunts and Ogres in front, the Death Knight to the rear. Protect this messenger of darkness as if the scenario depends on it—because it does.

✠ ✠ ✠ ✠ ✠ ✠

NOTE *Remember, the Death Knight's potent Death Coil has no effect on the Undead, so his roll in most Undead battles will be that of an interested observer. But don't worry, he'll make up for it elsewhere.*

✠ ✠ ✠

Fight through the first Undead ambush and regroup west of the village. Form a classic Grunts-in-front-Axethrowers-in-the-rear defense. Send the Knight to cast Death Coil on one of the Shipyard's defenders. It will probably kill the Human and cause the rest to charge. Run home with the Knight; when the guards hit your line they'll be decimated.

Head for the shipyard—don't sweat liberating the Farms. If you wander too far south you'll trigger another Undead ambush. Build a Transport, load everyone, and set sail for the island. Killing the Mage is Job One.

You can handle the remaining Undead in good time. Research Decay and Raise Dead, load the Transport, and steam north.

Offload all but one on the extreme north edge of the mainland's

Figure 3.17 *Assault on Mage Isle. Grunts hack away while the Undead stand around wondering what to do.*

eastern shore. Take the remaining passenger and land on the beach to the south. Move east of the woods and liberate the Trolls found there.

Once you get everyone back to the mainland, have the Death Knight cast Decay on the Elven Archers.

Then, to add insult to injury, raise them from the dead. Form up the troops to slaughter the Undead west of the Archers' former position. Follow up by Decaying the Tower and its attendant Archers, and using an Ogre to free the Orcs (he's fast enough to get out of town before what's left of the Tower gets him).

Back on the boat. Ferry the troops south to the next coastline opening. Keep them close to the water until you're ready to fight— as soon as they move inland some Humans with a very serious

Paladin attack. Don't unload the Death Knight. The Paladin will eat him for lunch.

March forward and give battle. After slaying the Humans, bring the Knight ashore. Again, destroy the Tower with Decay and move out. Capture the Blacksmith and Catapult. Upgrade everything except the Cat.

Continue hiking toward the Daemon, baiting and ambushing the foot troops you encounter. Use the Death Knight against the Ballistas and Towers but keep a sharp eye out for Paladins. Set up shop a little south of the Daemon's place. Repeatedly send the dark one to hit him with Death Coil. When you've sufficiently weakened the holder of the Jeweled Scepter of Sargeras, draw him into your line and stuff his body with upgraded axes. He ain't so bad.

Figure 3.18 *Laying it on the Elven Archers. The Death Knight casts Decay on the hapless longbowmen.*

Mission Ten

Alterac

Your capture of the Jeweled Scepter greatly pleases Ner'zhul. Word comes that you are to entrust it to the remaining warriors of the Bleeding Hollow clan; they are to return it to Draenor in all haste.

Deathwing and his Dragons deliver you to the Keep at Alterac. You could easily bring these curs to their knees, but they have hidden the tome you seek. They're also cunning enough to strike a bargain, knowing it's their only salvation. Should they tell you the location of the Book, however, they fear the retribution of the nations of Lordaeron and Stromgarde. They're willing to exchange the Book of Medivh for the destruction of these forces that sit along their borders.

You must eliminate the military outposts maintained by Lordaeron and Stromgarde. Then seal your pact by entering into Alterac, contacting the Human Mage who guards the Book, and escorting him to safety.

Marching Orders

- ✠ **Objectives:** Destroy the outposts belonging to Lordaeron and Stromgarde.Rescue the Mage from Alterac and return him to the Circle of Power.

- ✠ **Starting Location:** Northwest corner. (The Mage is in the southeast corner.)

- **Enemy Location:** Kul Tiras forces—between the rocks in a semicircle around the Orcs' starting position; Nation of Stromgarde—northeast corner; Lordaeron's troops—southwest.

- **Resources:** Eight Gold Mines—three evenly spaced, running northeast to southwest, in the rocks fronting the Orc's position; three more south, between the river and western map edge; one northeast; one in map center. Two Oil splotches—one at the river's bend; one at its southern end.

Running Metal Through Mortals

Despite the rescue-the-Mage wild card, this is a straightforward scenario. Your job is to kill Humies and flatten their dwellings. When the killing and flattening is done, bringing the Mage back to the Circle of Power is piece of cake.

Send everyone, I mean *everyone* (except two Peons) to clear the three detachments of Kul Tirasian soldiers located in the semicircular ring which surround your forces. Attack each in turn. If you're careful only the troops involved in the immediate skirmish will fight. Once you've slaughtered Humans, proceed to the Mine located north of the map's center and set up shop. Send an Ogre, two Knights, and a Dragon back to guard the main base.

Speaking of home base, have the Peons you left behind build a Lumber Mill, a pair of Pig Farms, and the obligatory Guard Towers. As funds permit, erect a Barracks and Great Hall. Yeah, it'll be tight, but you need the ability to reinforce from within. The computer takes awhile to wake up; however, once it does, it pays you regular house calls culminating in a charge by a herd of Knights.

METZEN · 96

Meanwhile, back at the center-screen ranch, the cash should be piling up. As soon as possible send a cadre of Peons to the Mine you passed en route to your current location. Build a Great Hall and start mining. You'll need everything but the kitchen sink to win this one, so you might as well generate the cash flow to handle it. Construct four Dragon Roosts, two Temples of the Damned, an Altar of Storms, and two Barracks in Center City.

🕱 🕱 🕱 🕱 🕱 🕱

TIP *If the Mines are unclaimed, construct a Guard Tower adjacent to them. Sometimes the computer attempts to mine gold without first securing the area. In this case, you can lay waste to a lot of enemy Peasants with a single Guard Tower. Now, if you feel really sneaky (not to mention wealthy), send a Death Knight to assist the Guard Tower. As the Tower kills Peasants the Death Knight can use Raise Dead to recruit them.*
Doesn't seem fair does it? But then, as I've said . . .

🕱 🕱 🕱

It's time to take out the wimps of Lordaeron. Use the standard tactics you've learned. First, secure the southern rock-belt Mine. Then, slowly advance with Cats and Death Knights in the lead. The Dragons will supply air support.

☒ ☒ ☒ ☒ ☒ ☒

TIP *Ogre Runes are particularly useful here. Cast them between the Cats and an opposing formation. When the Catapults fire the enemy charges, hoping to negate the threat to their front. Unfortunately for them, they walk into the Runes—killing most of the advancing Humans.*

☒ ☒ ☒

Secure the Lordaeron village and, as always, construct Cannon Towers to mop up for you. Stroll down to the river, fabricate a

Figure 3.19 *Guarding the home base gates*

Figure 3.20 *The raiding party*

Transport, and send some Knights, Ogres, and a Death Knight across for the Mage.

By landing on the southern shore you can avoid raising the ire of the Kul Tiras detachment at the northern end of the island. Escort the Mage to the Circle of Power with a couple of Grunts. By now the countryside should be safe for travel—at least for your side.

Two objectives down, one to go. The Nation of Stromgarde is a tough nut. They can't match your coin, however. Just take a little time to train a devastatingly powerful force, and then move in. Be methodical, conquer the city piece by piece, and don't forget to first soften the defenses with Cats, Dragons, and Death Knights.

Mission Eleven

The Eye of Dalaran

With the Book of Medivh in your control and the Jeweled Scepter delivered to Ner'zhul, only one artifact remains to be won. The Mages of Dalaran have created a device to focus their magiks in an effort to reconstruct the Violet Citadel. Ner'zhul desires this Eye of Dalaran to focus the dark powers of the underworld for the creation of his portals.

Teron Gorefiend has traveled to the Stronghold of the Human Mages at Cross Island, where they now rebuild their towers amid heavy fortifications. You must break through their shoreline defenses, establish a base, and capture the Eye of Dalaran. No walls will protect them from the vengeance of the Horde.

Marching Orders

- ✖ **Objectives:** Destroy all Mage Towers.
  Destroy all of Dalaran.

- ✖ **Starting Location:** Western island.

- ✖ **Enemy Location:** Forces of Dalaran—northeast and southeast corner; Nation of Lordaeron—coast and southwest.

- ✖ **Resources:** Four Gold Mines—north-center, south-center, southwest, mideast; two Oil splotches—one north, one south of center in the moat-like sea.

From the Halls of Montezuma

This scenario gives you a chance to conduct a classic amphibious invasion and beachhead expansion. Our story opens with the Orcish navy embroiled in a bitter battle for the Straits of Lordaeron. You'll probably win no matter how you click; nevertheless, it's important to keep as many of your ships afloat as possible. Concentrate on massing fires against a single target. Send the Dragons—when they're not targeting Gryphons—to attack Battleships.

After defeating the Humans, load the Transports and form one large flotilla, keeping the troop ships to the west. Slowly slide down the Lordaeron coast, taking out Towers as you go. When your task force approaches the southern edge of the first inland forest, land the Marines.

Figure 3.21 *Axethrowers guard the wooded path opened by the Peons.*

Figure 3.22 *The Orcish Hordes flow south toward Dalaran.*

Whisk by the woods, make camp on the east side, and let the Sappers blow the Aviary. Building a couple of Guard Towers is important once you buy the Lumber Mill. Otherwise, those white-feathered bird dudes will be all over you. Lay out the standard town stuff (make sure you have two Barracks early on), but watch the placement. Don't block the Peons' path to either the Great Hall or the Lumber Mill.

NOTE *As an alternative to the foregoing, land your troops just south of the second Lordaeron Tower (counting from the north) and build a Great Hall on*

the west side of the woods. Use Peons to cut a path
through the woods to the Gold Mine. This strategy has
the advantage of providing more room at the cost of a
slower buildup.

✠ ✠ ✠

As income permits, creep south.

After you have Ogre, Death Knight and Decay capabilities, fall on the Dalaran's southern village in earnest. It's really not too tough if you get there in the mid- to early part of the game. Consolidate forces, build Cats, train Death Knights and Dragons.

Before heading north to take out the Mage Towers, conduct a seven- to nine-strong Dragon strike on the Lordaerons massing to the west. This keeps them off your back while you get down to the serious business of destroying the Dalaran Mages.

Once you've seriously crippled their defenses, use Decay, Catapults and Dragons to take out the island's Mage Towers.

✠ ✠ ✠ ✠ ✠ ✠

CAUTION *Watch out for the Paladins. They're*
absolute death for your Knights. Work them over with
Cats, Dragons, or Ogres but never Death Knights.

✠ ✠ ✠

Mission Twelve

The Dark Portal

As the burning remains of your victims fill the air with acrid smoke, the sky fills with a figure as black as night. Deathwing descends, exhausted from his long journey from Grim Batol, bearing grave news from his brothers at Blackrock Spire.

The Alliance has sent a host of forces to the Black Morass and has engaged the forces of Warsong and the Shattered Hand at the Dark Portal. You must rally the forces of Shadowmoon to break through this siege, and return the artifacts you have secured to Draenor. Only then can Ner'zhul's plan of opening portals to new worlds be realized.

Succeed and you will command vast armies as they ravage untold worlds. Fail and be slaughtered.

Marching Orders

- ☒ **Objectives:** Capture the Dark Portal. Destroy all Humans.

- ☒ **Starting Location:** Northeast corner.

- ☒ **Enemy Location:** Nation of Azeroth—west-center; Nation of Kul Tiras—northeast corner; Nation of Dalaran—northwest corner; Nation of Lordaeron—southeast corner.

- ☒ **Resources:** Five Gold Mines—north-center, center, east-center, east edge, south-center, and west-center. Oil splotches—west, center, west-center.

The Grand Finale

First, let's get one thing straight: Don't attack those Towers to the south. They'll wipe you slick. Instead, send Deathwing over the forest on the east edge of the map. As he heads south you'll see two Towers. Use Deathwing, a Cat and some foot soldiers to destroy them both. March southeast along the edge of the eastern woods, where the forest meets the map edge. Blast a hole in the wall and continue south until you come to more foliage. Take care. If the traffic gets too congested your units will try to go the long way around—and stroll through the heart of the Alliance. Follow the trees west until you come to a Mine. Set up camp here.

Figure 3.23 *No, me first! The Orcs stream through the hole in the wall.*

Figure 3.24 *Final defenses at the forest gap during a typical attack*

Order the first military units on the scene to Stand across the forest gap west of the Mine. Other Orcs should guard the breach in the wall and the gap between the wall and northern forest. As soon as possible, build Farms to plug these holes. Sprinkle some Guard Towers in front of your units covering the gap between the north and south forests.

If you survive the initial Human attacks, start working on production. Buy into the typical upgrades and buildings. Eventually your economic output is high and the attack frequency low. It's the time to send an expedition to capture the Mine at the center of the map.

Send Dragons to destroy the buildings leading to this Mine. Don't mess with units on the other side of the southern gap. If you don't bother them, they won't bother you. When you come to the

Guard Towers, pound on them from a safe range with the Catapults. Once you get to the Mine, build a Town Hall, train some Peons, and start mining.

Once you have the second Mine pumping gold, pour through the gaps in the rocky ridge and conquer the Humans residing there. Unfortunately, the village Mines are empty, which raises the last significant obstacle to victory—gold depletion.

The Mines you have are all you'll get, so take it easy on those pricey Dragons and Death Knights. I prefer Catapults, anyway, because of their faster rate of fire.

Learn the layout of the rest of the map using the Ogre-Mage spell, Eye of Kilrogg. The Nation of Dalaran defends the three western islands. The Portal is on the center island. You'll see an Oil splotch in the southwest corner of the map; this is a safe place to build ships. Don't forget to erect Guard Towers to discourage the Gryphons from hanging around the naval buildings.

Attack the north island from the west with your Dragon swarm. This island has no Destroyers, no Guard Towers, and only a few Archers. Once you kill off the opposition, land your Catapults and their guard (Ogres, Grunts, and so on) to mop up the buildings.

The south island is trickier. It comes equipped with Dragon-slaying Guard Towers, Destroyers, and a Gryphon Aviary. Bombard the Aviary from the waterside to prevent ground units from assaulting you. Keep a Juggernaught available to deal with Destroyers, and a Dragon or two to handle Battleships.

Having destroyed the Manish Horde's ships and Aviary, level the Cannon Towers on the north side of the island. Land your troops, fend off any counterattacks, destroy buildings, and prepare for the final assault on the central island.

As before, use the Dragons to destroy the Cannon Tower. Lure the Gryphon out and over some of your Guard Towers. Then have fun as your Dragons enjoy a turkey shoot on the remaining units.

METZEN·96

Appendix

Cheats & Tables

Cheat Codes

To enable the Warcraft II cheat codes press "Enter" while playing and type the appropriate message.

Cheat	Code
Victory	Unite the clans
Loss	You pitiful worm
God	It is a good day to die
Cash	Glittering prizes
Oil	Valdez
Magic	Every little thing she does
Upgrade	Deck me out
Show Map	On Screen
Fast Build	Make it so
Finale	There can be only one
No Victory	Never a winner
Lumber	Hatchet
Enable Mission Jump	Tigerlily
Jump to Mission	Orc14, Human14, etc.
Special Sound Track	Disco

Table 1. Alliance Units

	PEASANT	FOOTMAN	ELVEN ARCHER	ELVEN RANGER	KNIGHT DEMOLITION SQUAD	PALADIN	BALLISTA
Visual Range:	4	4	5	6	4	5	9
Hit Points:	30	60	40	50	90	90	110
Magic Points:	–	–	–	–	–	255	–
Build Time:	45	60	70	70	90	90	250
Gold:	400	600	500	500	800	800	900
Lumber:	–	–	50	50	100	100	300
Oil:	–	–	–	–	–	–	–
Attack Range:	1	1	4	4	1	1	8
Armor:	–	2	0	0	4	4	0
Basic Damage:	3	6	3	3	8	8	80
Piercing Damage:	2	3	6	6	4	4	0
Effective Damage:	1–5	2–9	3–9	3–9	2–12	2–12	25–80
Speed:	10	10	10	10	13	13	5
Explosive Damage:	–	–	–	–	–	–	–

Table 2. Paladin Spells

Holy Vision	(70pts)	shows all terrain (& all enhabitants temporarily)
Healing	(6pts/hp)	heals wounded
Exorcism	(4pts/hp)	causes injury to enemy undead (can be cast on a group or single target)

MAGE	DWARVEN	GNOMISH FLYING MACHINE	GRYPHON RIDER	OIL TANKER	ELVEN DESTROYER	TRANSPORT	BATTLESHIP	GNOMISH SUBMARINE
9	4	9	6	4	8	4	8	5
60	40	150	100	90	100	150	150	60
255	–	–	–	–	–	–	–	–
120	200	65	250	50	90	70	140	100
,200	700	500	2,500	400	700	600	1,000	800
–	250	100	–	200	350	200	500	150
–	–	–	–	–	700	500	1,000	900
2	1	–	4	–	4	1	6	4
0	0	2	5	10	10	0	15	0
0	4	–	0	–	35	–	130	50
9	2	–	16	–	0	–	0	0
5–9	1–6	–	8–16	–	2–35	–	50–130	10–50
8	4	17	14	10	10	10	6	7
–	400	–	–	–	–	–	–	–

Table 3. Mage Spells

Lightning	(0pts)	bolts of energy will strike victim regardless of armor
Fireball	(100pts)	a ball of flame launches into its target
Slow	(50pts)	temporarily slows target in movement and reflex
Flame Shield	(80pts)	functions as a fiery barrier and weapon
Invisibility	(200pts)	makes caster and target invisible (any interaction other than movement terminates spell)
Polymorph	(200pts)	turns victim into a harmless animal
Blizzard	(25pts/area)	ice storm that can attack one target or large areas

Table 5. Units of the Orcish Horde

	PEON	GRUNT	TROLL AXE-THROWER	TROLL BERSERKER	OGRE	OGRE-MAGE	CATAPUL
Visual Range:	4	4	5	6	4	5	9
Hit Points:	30	60	40	50	90	90	110
Magic Points:	–	–	–	–	–	0	–
Build Time:	45	60	70	70	90	90	250
Gold:	400	600	500	500	800	800	900
Lumber:	–	–	50	50	100	100	300
Oil:	–	–	–	–	–	–	–
Attack Range:	1	1	4	4	1	1	8
Armor:	0	2	0	0	4	4	0
Basic Damage:	3	6	3	3	8	8	80
Piercing Damage:	2	3	6	6	4	4	0
Effective Damage:	1–5	2–9	3–9	3–9	2–12	2–12	25–80
Speed:	10	10	10	10	13	13	5
Explosive Damage:	–	–	–	–	–	–	–

Table 6. Ogre–Mage Spells

Eye of Kilrogg	(70pts)	conjures magical eye unit that acts like a Zeppelin but is fast
Bloodlust	(50pts)	affected will cause more damage to opponents
Runes	(200pts)	exploding trap (cannot decern friend from foe and also causes damage to adjacent areas)

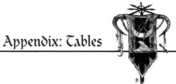

DEATH KNIGHT	GOBLIN SAPPER	ZEPPLIN	Dragon	OIL TANKER	TROLL DESTROYER	TRANSPORT	OGRE JUGGER-NAUGHT	GIANT TURTLE
9	4	9	6	4	8	4	8	5
60	40	150	100	90	100	150	150	60
255	–	–	–	–	–	–	–	–
120	200	65	250	50	90	70	140	100
1,200	700	500	2,500	400	700	600	1,000	800
–	250	100	–	200	350	200	500	150
–	–	–	–	–	700	500	1,000	900
3	1	–	4	–	4	–	6	4
0	0	2	5	10	10	0	15	0
–	4	–	0	–	35	–	130	50
9	2	–	16	–	0	–	0	0
5–9	1–6	–	8–16	–	2–35	–	50–130	10–50
8	11	17	14	10	10	10	6	7
–	400	–	–	–	–	–	–	–

Table 7. Death Knight Spells

Touch of Darkness	(0pts)	energy will strike victim regardless of armor
Death Coil	(100pts)	any coming in contact with it are robbed of energy which is given to the caster
Haste	(50pts)	temporarily speeds up target in movement and reflex
Raise Dead	(50pts/skeleton)	brings fallen soldiers back to life
Whirlwind	(100pts)	a damaging wind
Unholy Armor	(100pts)	uses one half of target's life force to make temporarily invunerable
Death and Decay	(25pts/area)	dark clouds that attack large areas

Table 8. Alliance Structures

	TOWN HALL	KEEP	CASTLE	FARM	BARRACK	ELVEN LUMBER MILL	BLACK- SMITH	SCOUT TOWER	GUAR TOWI
Visual Range:	4	6	9	3	3	3	3	9	9
Hit Points:	1,200	1,400	1,600	400	800	600	775	100	13(
Build Time:	255	200	200	100	200	150	200	60	14(
Gold Cost:	1,200	2,000	2,500	500	700	600	800	550	50(
Lumber Cost:	800	1,000	1,200	250	450	450	450	200	15(
Armor:	20	20	20	20	20	20	20	20	20
Production:	–	Gold 100+10	Gold 100+20	–	–	Lumber 100+25	–	–	–
Basic Damage:	–	–	–	–	–	–	–	–	4
Piercing Damage:	–	–	–	–	–	–	–	–	12
Effective Damage:	–	–	–	–	–	–	–	–	6–1

CANNON TOWER	STABLES	CHURCH	GNOMISH INVENTOR	MAGE TOWER	GRYPHON AVIARY	SHIPYARD	FOUNDRY	OIL REFINERY	OIL PLATFORM
9	3	3	3	3	3	3	3	3	3
160	500	700	500	500	500	1,100	750	600	650
190	150	175	150	125	150	200	175	225	200
1,000	1,000	900	1,000	1,000	1,000	800	700	800	700
300	300	500	400	200	400	450	400	350	450
20	20	20	20	20	20	20	20	20	20
–	–	–	–	–	–	–	–	Oil 100+25	–
50	–	–	–	–	–	–	–	–	–
0	–	–	–	–	–	–	–	–	–
10–50	–	–	–	–	–	–	–	–	–

Table 9. Orchish Structures

	GREAT HALL	STRONG-HOLD	FORTRESS	PIG FARM	BARRACK	TROLL LUMBER MILL	BLACK SMITH	SCOUT TOWER	GUARD TOWER
Visual Range:	4	6	9	3	3	3	3	9	9
Hit Points:	1,200	1,400	1,600	400	800	600	775	100	130
Build Time:	255	200	200	100	200	150	200	60	140
Gold Cost:	1,200	1,000	1,600	500	700	600	800	550	500
Lumber Cost:	800	1,000	1,200	250	450	450	450	200	150
Armor:	20	20	20	20	20	20	20	20	20
Production:	–	Gold 100+10	Gold 100+20	–	–	Lumber 100+25	–	–	–
Basic Damage:	–	–	–	–	–	–	–	–	4
Piercing Damage:	–	–	–	–	–	–	–	–	12
Effective Damage:	–	–	–	–	–	–	–	–	6–16

CANNON TOWER	OGRE MOUND	ALTAR OF STORMS	GOBLIN ALCHEMIST	TEMPLE OF THE DAMNED	DRGON ROOST	SHIPYARD	FOUNDRY	OIL REFINERY	OIL PLATFORM
9	3	3	3	3	3	3	3	3	3
160	500	700	500	500	500	1,100	750	600	650
190	150	175	150	125	150	200	175	225	200
1,000	1,000	900	1,000	1,000	1,000	800	700	800	700
300	300	500	400	200	400	450	400	350	450
20	20	20	20	20	20	20	20	20	20
–	–	–	–	–	–	–	–	Oil 100+25	–
50	–	–	–	–	–	–	–	–	–
0	–	–	–	–	–	–	–	–	–
10–50	–	–	–	–	–	–	–	–	–

Computer Game Books

1942: The Pacific Air War:
   The Official Strategy Guide $19.95
The 11th Hour: The Official Strategy Guide $19.95
The 7th Guest: The Official Strategy Guide $19.95
Aces Over Europe: The Official Strategy Guide $19.95
Across the Rhine: The Official Strategy Guide $19.95
Alone in the Dark 3: The Official Strategy Guide $19.95
Armored Fist: The Official Strategy Guide $19.95
Ascendancy: The Official Strategy Guide $19.95
Buried in Time: The Journeyman Project 2:
   The Official Strategy Guide $19.95
CD-ROM Games Secrets, Volume 1 $19.95
Caesar II: The Official Strategy Guide $19.95
Celtic Tales: Balor of the Evil Eye:
   The Official Strategy Guide $19.95
Cyberia: The Official Strategy Guide $19.95
Computer Adventure Games Secrets $19.95
Dark Seed II: The Official Strategy Guide $19.95
Descent: The Official Strategy Guide $19.95
DOOM Battlebook $19.95
DOOM II: The Official Strategy Guide $19.95
Dracula Unleashed: The Official Strategy
   Guide & Novel $19.95
Dragon Lore: The Official Strategy Guide $19.95
Dungeon Master II: The Legend of Skullkeep:
   The Official Strategy Guide $19.95
Fleet Defender: The Official Strategy Guide $19.95
Frankenstein: Through the Eyes of the Monster:
   The Official Strategy Guide $19.95
Front Page Sports Football Pro í95:
   The Official Playbook $19.95
Fury3: The Official Strategy Guide $19.95
Hell: A Cyberpunk Thriller:
   The Official Strategy Guide $19.95
Heretic: The Official Strategy Guide $19.95
I Have No Mouth, and I Must Scream:
   The Official Strategy Guide $19.95
In The 1st Degree: The Official Strategy Guide $19.95
Kingdom: The Far Reaches: The Official
   Strategy Guide $14.95
Kingís Quest VII: The Unauthorized
   Strategy Guide $19.95
The Legend of Kyrandia:
   The Official Strategy Guide $19.95
Lords of Midnight: The Official Strategy Guide $19.95
Machiavelli the Prince:
   Official Secrets & Solutions $12.95
Marathon: The Official Strategy Guide $19.95
Master of Orion: The Official Strategy Guide $19.95
Master of Magic: The Official Strategy Guide $19.95
Microsoft Arcade: The Official Strategy Guide $12.95
Microsoft Flight Simulator 5.1:
   The Official Strategy Guide $19.95
Microsoft Golf: The Official Strategy Guide $19.95
Microsoft Space Simulator:
   The Official Strategy Guide $19.95

Might and Magic Compendium:
   The Authorized Strategy
   Guide for Games I, II, III, and IV $19.95
Myst: The Official Strategy Guide $19.95
Online Games: In-Depth Strategies and Secrets $19.95
Oregon Trail II: The Official Strategy Guide $19.95
The Pagemaster:
   Official CD-ROM Strategy Guide $14.95
Panzer General: The Official Strategy Guide $19.95
Perfect General II: The Official Strategy Guide $19.95
Prince of Persia: The Official Strategy Guide $19.95
Prisoner of Ice: The Official Strategy Guide $19.95
Rebel Assault: The Official Insider's Guide $19.95
The Residents: Bad Day on the Midway:
   The Official Strategy Guide $19.95
Return to Zork Adventurer's Guide $14.95
Romance of the Three Kingdoms IV:
   Wall of Fire: The Official Strategy Guide $19.95
Shadow of the Comet:
   The Official Strategy Guide $19.95
Shannara: The Official Strategy Guide $19.95
Sid Meier's Civilization,
   or Rome on 640K a Day $19.95
Sid Meier's Colonization:
   The Official Strategy Guide $19.95
SimCity 2000: Power, Politics, and Planning $19.95
SimEarth: The Official Strategy Guide $19.95
SimFarm Almanac:
   The Official Guide to SimFarm $19.95
SimLife: The Official Strategy Guide $19.95
SimTower: The Official Strategy Guide $19.95
Stonekeep: The Official Strategy Guide $19.95
SubWar 2050: The Official Strategy Guide $19.95
Terry Pratchettís Discworld:
   The Official Strategy Guide $19.95
TIE Fighter: The Official Strategy Guide $19.95
TIE Fighter: Defender of the Empire:
   Official Secrets & Solutions $12.95
Thunderscape: The Official Strategy Guide $19.95
Ultima: The Avatar Adventures $19.95
Ultima VII and Underworld:
   More Avatar Adventures $19.95
Under a Killing Moon:
   The Official Strategy Guide $19.95
WarCraft: Orcs & Humans Official
   Secrets & Solutions $9.95
Warlords II Deluxe: The Official Strategy Guide $19.95
Werewolf Vs. Commanche:
   The Official Strategy Guide $19.95
Wing Commander I, II, and III:
   The Ultimate Strategy Guide $19.95
X-COM Terror From The Deep:
   The Official Strategy Guide $19.95
X-COM UFO Defense: The Official Strategy
   Guide $19.95
X-Wing: Collectorís CD-ROM:
   The Official Strategy Guide $19.95

TO ORDER BOOKS

Please send me the following items:

Quantity	Title	Unit Price	Total
_____	_____	$_____	$_____
_____	_____	$_____	$_____
_____	_____	$_____	$_____
_____	_____	$_____	$_____
_____	_____	$_____	$_____
_____	_____	$_____	$_____

Subtotal	$_____
7.25% Sales Tax (CA only)	$_____
8.25% Sales Tax (TN only)	$_____
5.0% Sales Tax (MD only)	$_____
7.0% G.S.T. Canadian Orders	$_____
Shipping and Handling*	$_____
TOTAL ORDER	$_____

*$4.00 shipping and handling charge for the first book, and $1.00 for each additional book.

By telephone: With Visa or MC, call 1-916-632-4400. Mon.–Fri. 9–4 PST. **By mail:** Just fill out the information below and send with your remittance to:

PRIMA PUBLISHING
P.O. Box 1260BK
Rocklin, CA 95677-1260

Satisfaction unconditionally guaranteed

Name _____

Address _____

City _____ State _____ Zip _____

Visa /MC# _____ Exp. _____

Signature _____